DEDICATION

To my amazing wife and family, may Saint Pier Giorgio Frassati and Saint Carlo Acutis look over and protect us.

Free Gift for Our Readers!

Thank you for reading 50 Saints for Kids.

We created a special bonus just for you!

Scan the QR code to download your FREE

Virtue Tracker, Feast Day Calendar, Patron Saint Tracker and Discussion Guide

This fun journal helps kids:

Remember the saints they learn about

Reflect on their favorite stories

Grow in faith and curiosity

Scan now and start your saint adventure!

Introduction

Once there was a boy who wanted to be brave.

Once there was a girl who wanted to do something great.

Once there was a kid who wondered... Does my life really matter?

"Once there was..." can go on forever. That's what makes stories so exciting.

Some stories are made up.

But the stories in this book are real.

They are about real people who lived in the real world—just like you.

Every great story needs a hero.

This book has fifty of them.

But here's the big surprise:

None of them was born a hero.

Some were poor. Some were rich. Some were shy. Some were scared. Some made mistakes. Some were kids and teenagers—just like you.

What made them special wasn't how they started.

It was a choice.

At some point in their lives—sometimes in a big moment, sometimes in a quiet one—they chose what mattered most. They chose to trust God. They chose to do what was right, even when it was hard.

And that's how they became saints.

In this book, you'll meet all kinds of people—boys and girls, men and women, kings and workers, students and missionaries. You'll see that holiness isn't just for one kind of person.

It's for everyone.

The courage that helped St. Joan of Arc lead an army can help you stand up for what's right.

The faith of St. Dominic Savio as a boy can help you in your daily life.

The love of St. Thérèse can grow in your heart too.

You are not too young.

You are not too ordinary.

You are not too late.

These stories prove it.

So read closely.

Stay curious.

And get ready...

Because one of these stories might be about who you can become.

How to Use This Book

You can read this book from start to finish, jump to any page, or follow along with special feast days. There's no wrong way to read it.

At the end of each chapter, you'll find three fun and helpful parts:

Virtue Spotlight — The good habit this saint practiced

Remember This — One simple idea to keep with you

Hero Mission — Something you can try today

There's also a Virtue Tracker in the back. Each time you complete a mission, you can check it off and see your progress!

One last thing:

Some of the saints in this book were kids and teenagers—just like you.

Pay extra attention to their stories.

They're not just special cases.

They're showing you what's possible.

CHAPTER 1

St. Michael the Archangel

COMMANDER OF HEAVEN'S ARMY

"The angel who threw the first punch and won."

Who is like God? | Virtue: Courage & Obedience

The Story

Before the world was made, before the first star lit up the sky, there was a battle in heaven.

God had created billions of beautiful angels to live with Him. Most of them loved God with their whole hearts. But one angel, the most powerful and beautiful of all, decided he didn't want to serve God anymore. His name was Lucifer, and he was filled with pride.

He looked at himself and thought, *I should be in charge. I should be God.*

Lucifer whispered his plan to other angels, and some of them listened. They turned away from God and followed Lucifer instead.

That's when Michael stepped forward.

Michael was one of God's top angels, what the Bible calls an archangel, which means "chief angel." When Lucifer started his rebellion, Michael wasn't scared. He gathered all the angels who stayed faithful to God and led them into battle.

Michael's battle cry became the most famous question in heaven: **"Who is like God?"** In Hebrew, that is *"Mi-ka-El!"* That's where his name comes from. It wasn't just a battle cry. It was an answer. Nobody is like God. Not Lucifer. Not anyone.

The battle was fierce, but Michael and the good angels won. Lucifer and his followers were thrown out of heaven forever. From that day on, Lucifer became known as Satan, the enemy of God and people.

Michael didn't win because he was stronger than Satan. He won because he was on God's side. And that made all the difference.

Today, Michael is still working. He guards God's people, helps souls get to heaven, and fights against evil. He's the commander of God's army, and he's on your side.

Virtue Spotlight: Courage & Obedience

Courage means doing the right thing even when it's

scary or hard. Michael could have stayed quiet when Lucifer rebelled, but he spoke up and acted.

Obedience means trusting and following God, even when you don't have all the answers. Michael didn't ask a million questions. He heard God's call and answered it.

In your life: Have you ever stood up for someone being treated unfairly? That's courage. Have you done your chores or homework even when you didn't feel like it? That's obedience. Both are heroic.

Remember This

When you're afraid, remember: the most powerful warrior in heaven is on your side.

Hero Mission

1. The next time someone is being picked on, be brave enough to say something kind or tell a trusted adult.

2. Say this prayer before bed: *"St. Michael, protect me tonight and keep me close to God."*

3. Write down one thing you're afraid of, then ask God and St. Michael to help you face it with courage.

Feast Day

September 29 — Called Michaelmas, this feast celebrates Michael together with the other archangels Gabriel and Raphael. Some families celebrate with a special meal or by learning about angels together.

CHAPTER 2

St. Joseph

THE QUIET GUARDIAN

"He never spoke a word in Scripture and did everything that mattered."

Protector of the Holy Family | Virtue: Humility & Obedience

The Story

Joseph had a plan. He was going to marry a wonderful young woman named Mary, build a home for her, and start a family. It was a simple, quiet plan, and Joseph was a simple, quiet man. He was a carpenter in a tiny town called Nazareth, and he was good at his work.

Then everything changed.

An angel came to Joseph in a dream and told him

something almost impossible to believe: Mary was going to have a baby, God's Son, and Joseph was chosen to be His earthly father. Joseph's job would be to protect them both.

Joseph could have walked away. He could have said, *This is too much. This isn't what I signed up for. But he didn't.*

He woke up from that dream and did exactly what the angel said.

When wicked King Herod wanted to hurt baby Jesus, another angel warned Joseph in a dream. In the middle of the night, Joseph packed up everything and rushed his family to safety in Egypt. No complaints. No delays. Just action.

When it was safe to return, an angel told Joseph again, and again, he obeyed immediately.

Joseph raised Jesus as his own son. He taught Him how to use a saw, shape wood, and build things that would last. He worked hard every single day to make sure Jesus and Mary had food, a home, and safety.

The whole time, Joseph never said a word that was recorded in the Bible. Not one. But everything he *did* spoke louder than any words.

That's what true strength looks like.

Virtue Spotlight: Humility & Obedience

Humility means knowing you don't have to be the loudest or most important person in the room.

Joseph let Jesus shine without ever trying to steal the spotlight.

Obedience means doing what you're asked, even when it's hard or unexpected.

In your life: Do you do what your parents ask without arguing? Do you sometimes let others go first? That's both humility and obedience, and Joseph shows us they're not weaknesses. They're superpowers.

Remember This

The greatest heroes aren't always the loudest ones. Sometimes they're the ones who just show up and do the work.

Hero Mission

1. Do a chore at home today without being asked, and don't tell anyone you did it.
2. Pray for the person in your family who works hardest to take care of you.
3. Write a thank-you note to someone who quietly does things for you that you don't always notice.

Feast Day

March 19 — The Solemnity of St. Joseph. There's also a second feast on May 1, celebrating Joseph as the patron of workers. Some families bake bread or share a special meal to honor him.

CHAPTER 3

St. Peter

THE ROCK

"He denied Christ three times and became the Church's first leader."

First Pope | Virtue: Courage & Faith

The Story

Peter was a fisherman. Not a priest, not a scholar, just a tough, sunburned man who smelled like fish and spent his days on a boat. His real name was Simon. But Jesus looked at him and said something surprising:

"From now on, you'll be called Peter." Peter means *rock.*

Jesus saw something in Peter that Peter didn't yet see in himself.

Peter became one of Jesus's closest friends. He was the first to say out loud, *"You are the Son of God!"* Jesus said that faith was the very rock on which the Church would be built. Big words. Big responsibility.

But here's the part that's hard to read.

On the night Jesus was arrested, Peter was terrified. Soldiers and crowds were everywhere. Three different people pointed at Peter and said, *"You were with Jesus, weren't you?"* And three times, Peter said, *"No. I don't even know Him."*

When Peter realized what he had done, he went outside and wept.

That could have been the end of the story. But it wasn't.

After Jesus rose from the dead, He came to Peter on the beach. He didn't yell at him. He didn't give up on him.
Instead, He asked Peter three times, once for each denial, *"Do you love me?"* And each time Peter said yes, Jesus gave him a mission: *"Feed my sheep. Take care of my people."*

Peter went on to lead the early Church with tremendous courage. He preached boldly, healed the sick, and eventually died for his faith in Rome, upside down on a cross, because he said he wasn't worthy to die the same way as Jesus.

The fisherman who was too scared to admit he knew Jesus became the boldest leader the Church ever had.

Virtue Spotlight: Humility & Obedience

Courage doesn't mean you're never afraid. Peter was terrified, and he still came back. Real courage means getting back up after you fall

Faith means trusting Jesus even when things get hard or scary.

In your life: Have you ever made a mistake and felt ashamed? Peter did too. Jesus forgave him. Jesus forgives you, too.

Remember This

Falling doesn't make you a failure. Staying down does. Jesus always gives us a chance to start again.

Hero Mission

1. If you've done something wrong lately, tell God you're sorry today and know that He forgives you.
2. Practice being brave: say something kind to someone you normally feel nervous around.
3. Learn one fact about St. Peter and share it with your family at dinner.

Feast Day

June 29 — The feast of **Sts. Peter and Pau** celebrated together. The Church marks this day with special Masses. St. Peter's Basilica in Rome, one of the biggest churches in the world, is built over the very place where Peter was buried.

CHAPTER 4

St. Paul

THE GREAT MISSIONARY

"He hunted Christians, then a light knocked him off his horse."

From Persecutor to Apostle | Virtue: Zeal & Fortitude

The Story

Saul of Tarsus was not a nice man, at least not at first.

He was smart, well educated, and deeply religious. But he was also convinced that Christians were dangerous troublemakers. So he made it his mission to stop them. He hunted them down, had them arrested, and even watched approvingly while the first Christian martyr, Stephen, was killed.

Saul thought he was doing God's work. He was wrong.

One day, Saul was riding the road to a city called Damascus to arrest more Christians. Without any warning, a blazing light from the sky knocked him right off his horse. He fell to the ground, blind and shaking.

Then he heard a voice: *"Saul, Saul, why are you persecuting me?"*

"Who are you?" Saul cried.

"I am Jesus."

Everything Saul believed flipped upside down in that moment. The Jesus he'd been fighting against was real. He was God. And He was speaking directly to Saul.

Saul was blind for three days. When his sight came back, he was a completely different person. He changed his name to Paul and became the most passionate, tireless missionary the world would ever see.

Paul traveled thousands of miles by ship and on foot, through storms and deserts. He was beaten, thrown in prison, shipwrecked, and left for dead. He never stopped. He started churches all over the known world and wrote letters to encourage them, letters that are now part of the Bible.

Paul didn't just change his mind. He changed the whole ancient world.

Virtue Spotlight: Humility & Obedience

Zeal means doing something with all your energy and passion. Paul didn't do anything halfway.

Fortitude means not giving up when things get hard. Paul faced shipwrecks, beatings, and prison, and kept going.

In your life: What's something you care about so much that you work hard at it even when it's tough? That fire is a gift from God. Use it for good.

Remember This

No one is too far from God to be changed, not even someone who starts on the wrong side.

Hero Mission

1. Look up one place St. Paul visited on a map, like Greece, Turkey, or Rome.

2. Write a short letter to a friend or family member telling them something you love about them.

3. Think of a habit or attitude in your own life you'd like to change, and ask God's help to work on it.

Feast Day

June 29 — Paul shares his feast day with St. Peter. His conversion is also celebrated on **January 25**, called the Feast of the Conversion of St. Paul.

CHAPTER 5

St. Stephen

THE FIRST MARTYR

"He prayed for the men throwing rocks at him as he died."

Deacon & Witness | Virtue: Courage & Forgiveness

The Story

After Jesus went back to heaven, His followers had a lot of work to do. The early Church was growing rapidly, and the apostles needed help caring for people, especially the poor and widows who had no one to provide for them.

So they chose seven helpers, called deacons. Stephen was one of them.

Stephen wasn't just a helper. He was full

of faith and the Holy Spirit, and he spoke about Jesus with such boldness and wisdom that no one could argue against him. He also performed miracles.

This made some powerful people very angry.

They grabbed Stephen, dragged him before the religious leaders, and accused him of terrible things. But Stephen wasn't afraid. He looked them straight in the eyes and told the whole truth about God's history with His people and how they had rejected Jesus, the Son of God.

When he finished speaking, the crowd was furious. But Stephen looked up toward heaven and saw something remarkable: Jesus, standing at the right hand of God.

"I can see heaven open," Stephen said, "and the Son of Man standing at God's right side!"

That was too much for the crowd. They covered their ears, rushed at him, and dragged him outside to stone him, to throw rocks at him until he died.

As the rocks hit him, Stephen knelt and prayed out loud for the very people hurting him: *"Lord, do not hold this sin against them."*

Those were almost the same words Jesus had said on the cross.

Stephen was the very first Christian martyr, the first person to die for believing in Jesus. And standing nearby, watching the whole thing, was a young man watching over the coats of the stone-throwers. His name was Saul. One day, he would become St. Paul.

Virtue Spotlight: Humility & Obedience

Courage means telling the truth even when it costs you everything. Stephen did exactly that.

Forgiveness is one of the hardest things a person can do, and Stephen showed one of the most striking examples of it in all of history.

In your life, is there someone who was mean to you or hurt your feelings? Forgiveness doesn't mean pretending it didn't happen. It means asking God to help you let go of the hurt.

Remember This

Forgiving someone who has hurt you is one of the bravest things you will ever do.

Hero Mission

1. Think of someone who has hurt your feelings. Say a quiet prayer asking God to bless them today.
2. Tell someone a truth that's hard to say, in a kind and brave way.
3. Read Acts 7 in the Bible (or ask a parent to read it with you). It's Stephen's whole story.

Feast Day

December 26 — The day right after Christmas. It's a reminder that being a follower of Jesus sometimes takes real bravery. Some countries celebrate this day with traditions of giving to people experiencing poverty, honoring Stephen's spirit of service.

NOTES

CHAPTER 6

St. John the Apostle

THE ONE WHO STAYED

"Every apostle ran. John stayed at the foot of the cross."

Beloved Disciple | Virtue: Loyalty & Perseverance

The Story

When Jesus was arrested, almost everyone ran.

His friends had promised to stand by Him. Peter had said he would die before he ever abandoned Jesus. But when the soldiers came with torches and swords in the middle of the night, the disciples scattered into the darkness.

All except one.

John, the youngest of the apostles, probably still a teenager, followed Jesus all the way to the foot of the cross. He stood there with Jesus's mother Mary, watching the most painful thing imaginable, and he did not leave.

John had been close to Jesus from the very beginning. He and his brother James were fishermen when Jesus called them. Jesus even gave them a nickname: *Sons of Thunder,* because they were passionate and full of energy.

But John was also the apostle Jesus loved in a special, tender way. At the Last Supper, John sat right next to Jesus. When Jesus was dying on the cross, He looked down and saw John and Mary standing together. And He gave them to each other.

"Woman, here is your son," He said to Mary, nodding toward John. "Here is your mother," He said to John.

From that moment on, John took care of Mary as his own mother.

After Jesus rose from the dead, John ran to the empty tomb and was the first to believe. He went on to preach for decades, wrote the Gospel of John, three letters, and the Book of Revelation.

While many of the other apostles were martyred, John lived to a very old age. He never stopped telling people about Jesus's love, even when he was too old and weak to walk. They say he was carried into church, where he would say the same thing every time:

"Little children, love one another."

Virtue Spotlight: Humility & Obedience

Loyalty means staying by someone's side even when it's hard or costly. John showed up when everyone else disappeared.

Perseverance means not giving up. John kept sharing Jesus's love his entire life.

In your life: Are you the kind of friend who sticks around when things are tough? That kind of loyalty is rare and precious.

Remember This

Real love isn't a feeling. It's showing up, especially when things are hard.

Hero Mission

1. Be a loyal friend today. Check on someone who might be having a hard time.
2. Write or draw something for someone you love, just to remind them you care.
3. Pray for the courage to stay close to Jesus even when it feels difficult or embarrassing.

Feast Day

December 27 — Just two days after Christmas. John is the patron saint of love, loyalty, and writers. Artists often show him with an eagle, a symbol of his vision of Jesus in his Gospel.

CHAPTER 7

St. Thomas the Apostle

The Doubter Who Went Furthest

"He doubted, then traveled further than any other apostle."

Apostle to India | Virtue: Honesty & Zeal

The Story

Thomas was honest. Maybe a little too honest sometimes, but God used that honesty in a remarkable way. Thomas was one of Jesus's twelve apostles. He wasn't flashy or famous. But there are three moments in the Gospels where Thomas speaks up, and every single one of them is unforgettable.

The first time Jesus decided to go back to Jerusalem, even though it was dangerous, Thomas said to the other disciples, *"Let's go too, so that we can die with him."* That's courage mixed with honesty.

But the moment Thomas is most famous for came after the Resurrection.

Jesus had appeared to the other disciples while Thomas was out. When Thomas came back, they told him the most exciting news in history: *"We've seen Jesus! He's alive!"*

Thomas crossed his arms. "I won't believe it unless I see the nail marks in His hands and touch them myself."

A week later, Jesus walked through a locked door and stood right in front of Thomas.

"Put your finger here," Jesus said gently, holding out His hands. *"Stop doubting and believe."*

Thomas looked at Jesus, nail marks and all, and said something beautiful:

"My Lord and my God."

Jesus said, *"You believe because you've seen me. Blessed are those who believe without seeing."*

Thomas didn't run from his doubt. He was honest about it. And Jesus met him right there.

After Pentecost, Thomas became one of the boldest missionaries of all. He traveled thousands of miles, all the way to India, to tell people about Jesus. That was an extraordinary journey in those days. He started churches there that still exist today.

The doubter went the furthest of them all.

Virtue Spotlight: Honesty & Zeal

Honesty means telling the truth about what you think and feel, even your questions and doubts. Thomas didn't pretend. Jesus honored that.
Zeal means going all-in once you know the truth. When Thomas believed, nothing could stop him.

In your life: Do you ever have questions or doubts about faith? That's okay. Bring them to God honestly, just like Thomas did.

Remember This

It's okay to ask hard questions. Jesus isn't afraid of your doubts, and He will meet you in them.

Hero Mission

1. Write down one question you have about God or faith, and ask a parent, teacher, or priest about it.
2. Find India on a map and consider how far Thomas traveled on foot and by boat to share his faith.
3. Pray this prayer: "Lord, help me trust You even when I don't understand everything."

Feast Day

July 3 — Thomas is the patron saint of India, architects, and people who have doubts. Churches in India trace their origins back to St. Thomas, nearly 2,000 years ago.

NOTES

CHAPTER 8

St. Mary Magdalene

The First Witness

"She was the first person Jesus appeared to after the Resurrection."

Apostle to the Apostles | Virtue: Love & Courage

The Story

Mary Magdalene had been through a lot before she ever met Jesus.

The Gospels tell us Jesus had healed her from something that had made her life very dark and broken. The moment Jesus freed her from it, her whole world changed. From that day on, she followed Jesus everywhere, through towns, up hillsides, across deserts.

She was there for His teachings. She was there when He healed people. And when most of His disciples ran away on the night He was arrested, Mary Magdalene stayed.

She was at the foot of the cross when Jesus died. She watched where they buried Him. And on the third day, before the sun had even fully risen, she went to the tomb with spices to anoint His body.

But the tomb was empty.

Mary stood outside crying. Two angels appeared and asked her, *"Why are you weeping?"*

"Because they have taken my Lord," she said, *"and I don't know where they've put Him."*

Then she turned around and saw a man she didn't recognize.

"Why are you crying?" He asked. *"Who are you looking for?"*

She thought He was the gardener. *"Sir, if you carried Him away, please tell me where He is."*

Then he said one word, just one, and it changed everything:

"Mary."

She knew that voice. She knew that name.

"Rabboni!" she cried. Teacher.

Jesus was alive. He had chosen Mary Magdalene to be the very first person to see Him, and He sent her to tell the apostles, making her the first person in history to announce the Resurrection.

Because of this, the Church has always called her the *Apostle to the Apostles,* the one who brought the most important news in the world to the men who would spread it everywhere.

Virtue Spotlight: Love & Courage

Love kept Mary Magdalene close to Jesus even when it hurt, through His death, burial, and early-morning grief.
Courage made her the one who showed up first, stayed the longest, and became the first herald of the Resurrection.

In your life: Love and loyalty look like showing up, even on hard days, even when it's sad, even when no one is watching.

Remember This

Jesus calls each of us by name, and when we hear His voice, everything changes.

Hero Mission

1. Do something kind for someone who is sad or grieving this week. Sit with them, draw a picture, or pray for them.

2. Tell someone some good news today. Practice being a messenger of joy.

3. Sit quietly for two minutes and imagine Jesus saying your name. What would you say back to Him?

Feast Day

July 22 — In 2016, Pope Francis elevated her feast to the same level as the apostles, honoring her role as the first witness to the Resurrection. She is the patron saint of penitents, converts, and hairdressers.

CHAPTER 9

St. Martha

The Faithful Servant

"She told Jesus exactly what she thought, and He loved her for it."

Friend of Jesus | Virtue: Diligence & Faith

The Story

Martha wasn't shy.

She and her siblings, Mary and Lazarus, were some of Jesus's closest friends. Whenever Jesus came to Bethany, He came to their house. Martha made sure everything was perfect. She cooked. She cleaned. She organized. She worked her hands to the bone to take care of everyone.

One day, Martha was bustling around

the kitchen while her sister Mary sat at Jesus's feet listening to Him talk. Martha had had enough. She marched right up to Jesus and said, *"Lord! Don't you care that my sister has left me to do all the work by myself? Tell her to come help me!"*

Most people would never speak to a rabbi like that. But Martha didn't hesitate.

Jesus answered her gently: *"Martha, Martha, you are worried and bothered about so many things. But only one thing is truly needed. Mary has chosen the better part, and it won't be taken from her."*

Jesus wasn't saying hard work is bad. He was saying, "Don't let busyness crowd out the most important thing: being with Him."

Martha heard Him. And she proved just how deep her faith ran a little while later.

Her brother Lazarus got very sick and died. By the time Jesus arrived, Lazarus had been in the tomb for four days. Martha ran out to meet Jesus with tears on her face and said one of the greatest statements of faith in the entire Bible:

"Lord, if You had been here, my brother would not have died. But even now, I know that whatever You ask of God, God will give You."

Jesus raised Lazarus from the dead that day. And it was Martha's faith that set the stage for one of His greatest miracles.

Virtue Spotlight: Diligence & Faith

Diligence means working hard and giving your best to whatever you do. Martha served with her whole heart.

Faith means trusting God even in the middle of grief and confusion, even when things go wrong.

In your life: Do you give your best effort to the tasks in front of you, homework, chores, helping out, even when it's tiring?

Remember This

Work hard and serve others, but never get so busy that you forget to spend time with Jesus.

Hero Mission

1. Help prepare or clean up after a meal at home without being asked.
2. Take five minutes today to sit quietly and just talk to Jesus, no distractions.
3. Next time something goes wrong, try saying a "Martha prayer": "Lord, I trust You, even now."

Feast Day

July 29 — Martha shares her feast day with her siblings, Mary and Lazarus. She is the patron saint of cooks, servers, hotel workers, and all who work hard to serve others.

CHAPTER 10

St. Anne

The Grandmother of God

"She prayed for a child her whole life. She became Jesus's grandmother."

Mother of Mary | Virtue: Patience & Faith

The Story

Anne and her husband Joachim had a wonderful life, except for one deep sadness. No matter how much they prayed, they could not have children. In the ancient world, this was considered a great sorrow, even a shame. People whispered about them. Some thought God must be displeased with them.

But Anne and Joachim never stopped praying.

Year after year, they asked God for a child. Year after year, they held on to hope even when it felt impossible. They were faithful, generous people who gave to the poor and worshipped God with their whole hearts, even without the answer they were longing for.

Then one day, after many long years of waiting, an angel appeared to Anne with extraordinary news: she would have a child. A daughter. And that daughter would be something the world had never seen before.

Anne's daughter was Mary, the young woman who would say yes to God, carry the Son of God in her womb, and become the Mother of Jesus.

That means Anne was Jesus's grandmother.

The same hands that held baby Mary would one day hold baby Jesus. The same woman who sang little Mary to sleep raised the girl who would say the most important "yes" in history.

We don't know everything about Anne's life because most of what we know comes from early Christian tradition rather than the Bible itself. But the Church has always honored her as a model of persevering prayer, of someone who kept asking, kept believing, and kept trusting God's timing even when it seemed too late.

Anne teaches us that unanswered prayers aren't forgotten prayers. Sometimes God is preparing something far greater than we imagined.

Virtue Spotlight: Patience & Faith

Patience means trusting God's timing even when the waiting is really hard. Anne waited years before her prayer was answered.

Faith means believing God is good even when things don't go the way you hoped or planned.

In your life: Is there something you've been praying for that hasn't happened yet? You're in good company. Keep praying. Keep trusting.

Remember This

God never forgets your prayers. Sometimes, he's just preparing something even more wonderful than you asked for.

Hero Mission

1. Write down one prayer you've been praying for a long time. Ask St. Anne to pray alongside you.
2. Do something kind for a grandparent or older adult in your life today.
3. Plant something small, a seed or a flower, as a reminder that good things take time to grow.

Feast Day

July 26 — Anne shares her feast with Joachim, her husband. She is the patron saint of grandmothers, mothers, homemakers, and those who are waiting on God's answer to a long prayer. Many churches around the world are named in her honor.

NOTES

CHAPTER 11

St. George

The Knight Who Faced the Emperor

"Before the dragon, he faced something harder. the emperor."

Patron of England | Virtue: Courage & Faith

The Story

Most people know St. George as the knight who slew the dragon. But the real story is even more remarkable, and it didn't involve a dragon at all.

George was a soldier in the Roman army, and a good one. He was well-trained, respected, and on his way to a promising career. There was just one problem. The Roman Emperor Diocletian, one of the cruelest rulers in history, had decided that Christians were enemies of the empire. He ordered every soldier to make a sacrifice to the Roman gods and deny Christ. Anyone who refused would be executed.

George refused.

He stood before the emperor himself and declared that he was a Christian. He knew exactly what that meant. He wasn't naïve or careless. He made his choice with full knowledge of what it would cost him.

The emperor tried everything to make George change his mind. He offered him land, money, and a place of honor. George said no every time. So Diocletian ordered him tortured and, when George still wouldn't deny his faith, had him executed on April 23 in the year 303.

George died not on a battlefield, but in a courtyard, standing firm under pressure that would have broken most people. No sword, no armor. Just faith.

The dragon story came later, attached to his legend over the centuries. In the old telling, George rescues a town from a fearsome dragon by making the sign of the cross and striking it down. Whether taken as legend or symbol, the meaning is the same: George faced monsters, real and imagined, and he never ran.

He became the patron saint of England, soldiers, and dozens of other countries because his story speaks to something universal. Sometimes the greatest battle isn't out on a field. It's in a room, alone, when someone powerful tells you to be someone you're not.

George said no.

Virtue Spotlight: Courage & Faith

Courage means holding to what you believe, even when the cost is severe. George had everything to lose and chose his faith anyway.

Faith means trusting God more than you trust power, comfort, or safety.

In your life: Has anyone ever pressured you to act against what you know is right? That moment, however small, is your version of what George faced.

Remember This

The bravest thing you can do is stay true to who you are when someone powerful tells you to be someone else.

Hero Mission

1. Think of one belief or value you hold. What would it look like to stand up for it this week?
2. Learn one fact about the country or cause St. George is patron of and share it with someone.
3. Pray this prayer: *"Lord, give me the courage to be honest about who I am, even when it's hard."*

Feast Day

April 23 — St. George's feast is celebrated with particular joy in England, where he is the national patron saint. The red cross of St. George on a white background forms part of the British flag.

NOTES

CHAPTER 12

St. Sebastian

The Soldier Who Wouldn't Stay Down

"Shot with arrows and left for dead – he walked back in."

Arrow Survivor | Virtue: Fortitude & Courage

The Story

Sebastian had a plan, and it was a bold one.

He joined the Roman imperial guard not to serve the emperor, but to secretly help Christians who were being arrested and killed for their faith. From inside the palace, he could visit prisoners, encourage them before they died, and make sure they weren't abandoned.

For a while, it worked. Sebastian moved freely through the

palace, trusted by the emperor, quietly doing what he could for people the empire had condemned.

Then someone found out.

Emperor Diocletian was furious. He saw Sebastian's secrecy as the worst kind of betrayal. He ordered Sebastian tied to a post and used as target practice for archers. The soldiers shot him with so many arrows that witnesses said he looked like a porcupine. They left him for dead.

He wasn't dead.

A Christian woman named Irene went to retrieve his body for burial and found him still alive. She took him in and nursed him back to health. When Sebastian recovered, his friends begged him to leave Rome and go somewhere safe. He had been given a second chance at life. Most people would have taken it.

Sebastian walked back into the palace.
He found the emperor and confronted him face to face, calling on him to stop persecuting Christians. Diocletian, stunned that Sebastian was even alive, ordered him beaten to death and thrown in the sewer.

Sebastian is remembered not just for surviving the arrows but for what he did with his survival. He didn't escape. He went back. That kind of courage is almost impossible to understand, but it came from one place: he believed in something more important than his own safety.

Virtue Spotlight: Fortitude & Courage

Fortitude means enduring pain, danger, or hardship

without giving up. Sebastian endured the arrows. Then he endured even more.

Courage is choosing the right thing even when you've already seen what it costs.

In your life: Have you ever had to do something hard twice because the first time didn't go the way you hoped? Doing it again anyway is exactly what Sebastian did.

Remember This

A second chance isn't always meant for escape. Sometimes it's meant for going back.

Hero Mission

1. Think of something you gave up on too soon. Is there a way to try again?
2. Do something kind for someone going through a hard time today, even if it's inconvenient.
3. Pray this prayer: *"Lord, give me the strength to keep going when I feel like stopping."*

Feast Day

January 20 — St. Sebastian is the patron saint of soldiers, athletes, and those who are sick. He is often shown in art with arrows, a reminder of his extraordinary survival and the faith that kept him standing.

CHAPTER 13

St. Lawrence

The Deacon Who Laughed at Death

"He was roasted alive. Halfway through, he told them to flip him over."

Treasurer of the Poor | Virtue: Courage & Joy

The Story

Lawrence was a deacon in Rome in the year 258, and his job was an important one. He was in charge of the Church's treasury, which meant he managed the money and goods used to help the poor.

When Emperor Valerian decided to crack down on Christianity, he had the Pope executed first. Before dying, Pope Sixtus II turned to Lawrence, who was weeping at his side, and told him not to grieve. "In three days," the pope said, "you will follow me."

Then the Roman prefect came for Lawrence. He had heard that the Church kept a great treasure, and he wanted it. He gave Lawrence three days to gather all the Church's wealth and hand it over.

Lawrence agreed.

He spent those three days visiting every corner of Rome. He went to the hospitals, the shelters, and the streets. He found the sick, the lame, the blind, and the poor, every person the Church had been caring for, and he brought them all together. When he appeared before the prefect on the third day, he gestured to the crowd behind him and said:

"Here is the treasure of the Church."

The prefect was not amused. He ordered Lawrence executed, slowly, on a gridiron over burning coals.

What happened next became one of the most famous moments in early Christian history. After a long time on the gridiron, Lawrence looked up at his executioners and said, with a calm smile: *"Turn me over. I'm done on this side."*

It wasn't defiance. It was something deeper. Lawrence had so thoroughly given his life over to God that even death couldn't shake his peace.

Virtue Spotlight: Courage & Joy

Courage in Lawrence wasn't loud or angry. It was steady and even cheerful, which made it all the more extraordinary.

Joy doesn't mean everything is easy. It means you have peace inside that circumstances can't touch.

In your life: Can you think of a time when you stayed calm or even found something to smile about in a hard situation? That's the beginning of Lawrence's kind of strength.

Remember This

Real joy isn't about your circumstances. It's about what's living in your heart that nothing can take away.

Hero Mission

1. Do something kind for someone who is poor or left out today, even something small.
2. The next time something frustrating happens, try to find one thing to be grateful for in the middle of it.
3. Pray this prayer: *"Lord, give me a joy that doesn't depend on things going my way."*

Feast Day

August 10 — St. Lawrence is the patron saint of cooks, comedians, and people with low incomes. Some families mark his feast day by giving to a food pantry or serving a meal to someone in need.

CHAPTER 14

St. Tarcisius

The Altar Boy Who Protected the Eucharist

"He died rather than let a mob touch what he was carrying."

Patron of Altar Servers | Virtue: Faith & Fortitude

The Story

Tarcisius was a young boy, probably around twelve years old, living in Rome during one of the most dangerous periods for Christians in history.

Christians were being arrested and executed, and those in prison were often cut off from the sacraments before they died. Someone needed to bring the Eucharist, the consecrated bread

that Catholics believe is truly the Body of Christ, from the church to the prisoners so they could receive it one last time.
It was too dangerous to send an adult. The roads were watched. A boy might slip through unnoticed.

Tarcisius volunteered.

He made his way through the streets of Rome carrying the Eucharist close to his chest, hidden beneath his clothing. For a while, it seemed like he would make it. Then a group of pagan boys spotted him. They recognized him as a Christian and demanded to know what he was carrying. They wanted to see it, to mock it, to take it from him.

Tarcisius refused to hand it over. He held it against himself as they attacked him.

By the time a Christian soldier named Quadratus drove the mob away, Tarcisius was badly hurt. He was carried to safety, but he died from his injuries shortly after. When people looked at what he had been protecting, they found the Eucharist unharmed.

Tarcisius never made it to the prisoners. But what he gave those prisoners, and everyone who heard his story after, was something more lasting: proof that faith isn't only for adults, and that something can be worth protecting with everything you have.

Virtue Spotlight: Faith & Fortitude

Faith means believing so completely in something that you act on it even at great cost. Tarcisius believed in what he was carrying.

Fortitude means holding on under pressure. Tarcisius held on.

In your life: Is there something you believe in strongly enough to protect, even when it's hard? Your faith is worth that kind of care.

Remember This

You don't have to be grown-up to be brave. Age has nothing to do with it.

Hero Mission

1. If you serve at your church in any way, do it with extra care and attention this week.
2. Think about what the Eucharist means to you. Write down one thought or question about it.
3. Pray this prayer: *"Lord, help me treat holy things as truly holy."*

Feast Day

August 15 — St. Tarcisius shares his feast day with the Assumption of Mary. He is the patron saint of altar servers and first communicants, a reminder that young people have always had a place of honor in the Church.me."

CHAPTER 15

St. Polycarp

The Bishop Who Wouldn't Flinch

"At 86, he said: 'He has never done me wrong. I will not deny Him.'"

Disciple of St. John | Virtue: Faith & Fortitude

The Story

Polycarp had known Jesus's own apostles. As a young man, he had sat at the feet of St. John, the beloved disciple, and learned the faith directly from someone who had walked with Jesus, eaten with Him, and watched Him die and rise again.

For decades, Polycarp served as the bishop of Smyrna, a city in what is now Turkey. He was known for his gentleness, his clarity, and his deep faithfulness. He was, by every account, a good man who had lived a long and holy life.

When he was 86 years old, the Roman authorities came for him.

A mob had been demanding Christian blood, and Polycarp's name was called. He was brought before the Roman proconsul and given a simple choice: curse Christ and go free, or refuse and be burned alive.

The proconsul tried to be reasonable. "What harm is it," he said, "to just say 'Caesar is Lord' and offer a little incense? Think of your age. Save yourself."

Polycarp was quiet for a moment. Then he spoke, calmly and without a tremor:

"Eighty-six years I have served Him. He has never done me wrong. How can I blaspheme my King who saved me?"

They burned him. Witnesses who wrote down the account said the flames seemed to form an arc around him rather than consume him, and that he stood in the middle of the fire like gold being refined, until the soldiers finally ended it by sword.

Polycarp was the last living link to the apostles. When he died, he carried something precious with him: a firsthand chain of memory that ran all the way back to Jesus Himself. He gave his life rather than break it.

Virtue Spotlight: Faith & Fortitude

Faith that has lasted 86 years is not the same as

faith in its first year. Polycarp's faith had been tested, deepened, and proven over a lifetime.

Fortitude means holding your ground when everything says to give way.

In your life: Faithfulness built over years is worth more than a burst of feeling that fades. Every day you choose to do the right thing is one more brick in that wall.

Remember This

A faith that lasts a lifetime is built one ordinary day at a time.

Hero Mission

1. Ask an older person in your life about their faith. How long have they believed? What has kept them going?
2. Do one small act of faithfulness today, something quiet that only you and God know about.
3. Pray this prayer: "Lord, help me serve You for my whole life, not just when it's easy."

Feast Day

February 23 — St. Polycarp is one of the earliest Christian martyrs whose story is recorded in detail by eyewitnesses. His feast is celebrated as a reminder that faithful, quiet endurance is its own kind of heroism.

CHAPTER 16

St. Agnes

The Girl Who Said No to an Empire

"She was 12 years old. Rome offered her the world. She refused."

Patron of Girls & Purity | Virtue: Courage & Purity

The Story

Agnes was twelve years old, and she was already attracting attention she didn't want.

She was a young Christian girl in Rome, and she had quietly made a promise to God: she would give her whole life to Him. That wasn't unusual for devout young Christians. What was unusual was what happened when a powerful Roman nobleman's son decided he wanted to marry her.

Agnes said no.

He sent her gifts. She refused them. He sent his father to plead her case. She still refused. He reported her to the Roman authorities as a Christian, hoping the threat of punishment would change her mind.

It didn't.

Agnes was brought before the prefect, who tried threats and then torture to break her resolve. When nothing worked, he sent her to a place intended to shame and humiliate her into compliance. Throughout it all, witnesses wrote that she remained calm, peaceful, and unafraid, as if protected by something no one could see.

Eventually, the prefect ordered her execution. Agnes died around the year 304, her faith intact.

She was barely older than some of the children reading this book.

The early Church was stunned and moved by her story. St. Ambrose, one of the great teachers of the early Church, wrote about her: she was too young to face death, he said, and yet she faced it without fear. She had something the empire couldn't give and couldn't take.

Her name in Latin means "pure" or "lamb." Every January 21, two lambs are brought to the church in Rome named after her, and their wool is eventually woven into the garments worn by archbishops worldwide—something small and gentle, lasting.

Virtue Spotlight: Courage & Purity

Courage doesn't always look like a soldier on a battlefield. Sometimes it looks like a twelve-year-old girl who simply refuses to be moved.

Purity means keeping your heart and your commitments clean and whole, even under pressure.

In your life: Have you ever been pressured to do something you knew was wrong, just to make someone else happy? Saying no takes real strength.

Remember This

You don't have to say yes to everything the world offers you. Some things are worth saying no to.

Hero Mission

1. Think of one area of your life where you feel pressure to compromise what you believe. Ask God to help you hold firm.
2. Do something gentle and kind for someone younger than you today.
3. Pray this prayer: *"Lord, help me keep my heart for You, no matter what I'm offered."*

Feast Day

January 21 — St. Agnes is the patron saint of girls, students, and those seeking purity of heart. Her feast day falls in the cold of January, yet the Church has always celebrated her with warmth, because her courage brings light to dark days.

CHAPTER 17

St. Lucy

The Girl Who Lit the Dark

"She gave away her dowry to the poor. Her suitor reported her to Rome."

Patron of the Blind | Virtue: Courage & Generosity

The Story

Lucy had a plan to give everything away.

She was a young Christian woman in Syracuse, Sicily, around the year 300. Her father had died and left her a sizable inheritance, money intended as her dowry, the gift a bride brought to her marriage. Lucy had other ideas. She wanted to give it all to people experiencing poverty.

Her mother was ill, and Lucy had been

praying at the tomb of St. Agatha, asking for her mother's healing. Her mother recovered. In gratitude, Lucy told her mother what she wanted to do with the inheritance. Her mother agreed.

There was just one problem. Lucy was already promised to a young pagan nobleman, and he expected that dowry. When Lucy began giving away her wealth, piece by piece, to people in need, her suitor noticed. He was furious. He reported her to the Roman governor as a Christian.

The governor ordered Lucy to offer a sacrifice to the Roman gods. She refused. He threatened to send her to a place of degradation. She told him that no one could corrupt a soul that didn't consent. When soldiers came to take her away, witnesses reported that something made it impossible to move her, as if she had been made immovable by something greater than physical force.

Eventually, she was condemned and executed by sword in the year 304.

Lucy means "light." Her feast falls on December 13, close to the shortest, darkest days of the year in the northern hemisphere. In Scandinavian countries, girls dress in white with candles on their heads to honor her, carrying light into the darkness of winter. It is exactly the right image for a young woman who chose to give rather than keep, and who faced the dark without flinching.

Virtue Spotlight: Courage & Generosity

Courage means acting on your convictions even when it puts you in danger. Lucy's generosity is what set everything in motion, and she never backed down from it.

Generosity means giving freely, even when it costs you something real.

In your life: Is there something you're holding onto that you could share with someone who needs it more? Generosity isn't just about money. Time, kindness, and attention count too.

Remember This

Giving freely is an act of courage. It means you trust God more than you trust what you're holding.

Hero Mission

1. Give something away today, your time, something you own, or a kind word, to someone who needs it.
2. Look up the tradition of St. Lucy's Day in Sweden or Norway and learn how they celebrate it.
3. Pray this prayer: *"Lord, help me be generous even when it's hard to let go."*

Feast Day

December 13 — St. Lucy is the patron saint of blind people, those with eye disease, and anyone who needs light in dark times. Her name and her feast day are a promise that light always comes back.

CHAPTER 18

St. Perpetua

The Mother in the Arena

"She was a young mother. She walked into the arena singing."

Martyr of Carthage | Virtue: Courage & Faith

The Story

Perpetua was twenty-two years old, a noblewoman in the city of Carthage in North Africa, and she had just given birth.

She was also a Christian, and in the year 203, the Roman Emperor Septimius Severus had banned any new conversions to Christianity. Perpetua had recently been baptized. She was arrested, along with several others, and awaited execution.

What makes Perpetua's story so extraordinary is that we have it in her own words. She kept a diary from inside prison, one of the earliest pieces of writing we have from a Christian woman. She wrote about nursing her baby through the prison bars. She wrote about her father, who came to beg her again and again to deny her faith to save her life. She wrote about the visions she received that gave her peace.

Her father's visits were the hardest part. He wept. He showed her the baby. He knelt at her feet. He did everything a loving father could do to change her mind.
Perpetua loved him deeply. But she told him the truth each time: she could not call herself something she wasn't.

She wrote down a moment when she pointed to a water jug and asked her father: "Can that jug be called anything other than what it is?" He said no. She said: "Neither can I call myself anything other than a Christian."

On the day of her execution, she and her companions walked into the arena singing hymns. Witnesses said she directed the executioner's sword herself, calmly and with grace.

Perpetua's courage was not the absence of love for her father or her child. It was love for God that ran even deeper. She held both, and she didn't pretend the choice was easy.

Virtue Spotlight: Courage & Faith

Courage sometimes means disappointing the people you love most to be faithful to God.

Faith is what Perpetua stood on when everything else in her life was pulling her in the other direction.

In your life: Have you ever had to make a hard choice between what someone you love wanted and what you knew was right? That is one of the hardest tests anyone faces.

Remember This

Being true to God doesn't mean you stop loving people. It means you love them honestly.

Hero Mission

1. Write a short note or prayer for a family member you love. Thank God for them.
2. Think of one thing you know is right that you've been avoiding because it's hard. Take one small step toward it today.
3. Pray this prayer: *"Lord, give me the courage to be honest, even when honesty costs me something."*

Feast Day

March 7 — St. Perpetua is celebrated along with her companion St. Felicity, a slave woman who was executed with her. Their feast is a reminder that courage belongs to everyone, regardless of age, rank, or background.

CHAPTER 19

St. Cecilia

The Patron of Music

"She sang to God in her heart even on her wedding day – and died for it."

Musician Martyr | Virtue: Courage & Joy

The Story

Cecilia came from a noble Roman family, and she had made a private vow to God: she would remain completely dedicated to Him. Then her parents arranged for her to marry a pagan nobleman named Valerian.

On her wedding day, surrounded by the music of celebration, Cecilia sang to God silently in her heart. The Latin phrase that describes this moment, cantantibus organis, meaning "while the instruments were playing," has made her the patron of music for centuries. She brought her inner life with her into the most public moment and kept them inseparable.

On her wedding night, Cecilia told Valerian about her vow and her faith. She spoke to him with such sincerity that instead of being angry, he was moved. He asked to know more. Eventually, both Valerian and his brother Tiburtius became Christians and began helping the poor and burying martyrs, which was illegal and dangerous work.

All three of them were eventually arrested. Valerian and Tiburtius were executed. Then the authorities came for Cecilia.

She was condemned to die, but the execution was botched. The executioner struck her three times with a sword and could not finish the job. She lived for three more days, during which she gave away everything she owned and asked a bishop to convert her home into a church.

She died in the early third century, young, joyful, and undefeated.

What stays with people about Cecilia is the singing. Not on a stage, not for anyone to hear. In her heart, while the world around her celebrated something else entirely. She had learned to carry God everywhere, into rooms where no one expected Him, into moments that didn't belong to Him on the surface.

That's what made her extraordinary.

Virtue Spotlight: Courage & Joy

Courage in Cecilia looked like refusing to let the outside world determine her inner life.

Joy means having a song inside you that circumstances can't silence.

In your life: Is there something you love, a song, a prayer, a quiet habit, that connects you to God in the middle of ordinary life? Hold onto it.

Remember This

You can carry God into any room. You don't have to leave Him at the door.

Hero Mission

1. Pick a song you love and listen to it today with the intention of offering it to God.
2. Think of one ordinary moment in your day, a meal, a walk, a quiet minute, and try to bring God into it.
3. Pray this prayer: *"Lord, help me carry You into every part of my day, even the parts that seem too ordinary."*

Feast Day

November 22 — St. Cecilia is the patron saint of musicians, singers, and music teachers. Her feast day is celebrated in music schools and churches around the world. Many choirs perform concerts in her honor to mark the day.

CHAPTER 20

St. Benedict

The Man Who Rebuilt Civilization

"He walked into a cave. What grew around him saved Western civilization."

Father of Western Monasticism | Virtue: Prudence & Faith

The Story

Benedict was done with Rome.

He had gone there as a young man to study, as ambitious young Romans did, and what he found there disgusted him. The city was loud, corrupt, and interested in almost everything except God. So Benedict walked away from his studies, left his friends behind, and went looking for silence.

He found it in a cave

above a lake outside the town of Subiaco. For three years, he lived there alone, praying, fasting, and thinking. A monk from a nearby monastery brought him food by lowering it down on a rope. That was his whole world.

Other men found him eventually. They wanted what he had. Could he teach them? Could he lead them? He tried, and it didn't always go well. One community he led actually tried to poison him because his standards were too demanding. Benedict left them and started again.

Over time, he built something that worked: a network of monasteries governed by a simple document called the Rule of St. Benedict. It wasn't harsh or complicated. It organized a monk's day around prayer, work, and study, in that order. Work was holy. Rest was necessary. Hospitality to strangers was required. Learning mattered.

When the Roman Empire collapsed and much of Europe fell into chaos, it was these monasteries that kept the lights on. Monks copied books by hand, educated children, cared for the sick, and preserved the accumulated knowledge of the ancient world through centuries of instability. The Rule that Benedict wrote in a cave in the sixth century shaped European civilization for a thousand years.

He didn't set out to save the world. He set out to find God. The world got saved in the process.

Virtue Spotlight: Prudence & Faith

Prudence means thinking carefully before you act and building things that last. Benedict didn't rush. He designed something wise, and it held together for centuries.

Faith means trusting that small, faithful things done well have consequences you can't always see.

In your life: Do you do your work carefully, even when no one is watching? That kind of faithfulness adds up.

Remember This

You don't have to change the world on purpose. Do the right things faithfully, and let God handle the rest.

Hero Mission

1. Organize one part of your day, schoolwork, chores, or prayer, more deliberately than usual.

2. Learn what the phrase "ora et labora" means and think about how it could apply to your own life.

3. Pray this prayer: *"Lord, help me do ordinary things with great faithfulness."*

Feast Day

July 11 — St. Benedict is the patron saint of Europe, monks, and students. His medal, bearing his initials and a cross, is one of the most widely used sacramentals in the Catholic Church.

CHAPTER 21

St. Augustine of Hippo

The Wild Boy Who Became a Doctor

"He ran from God for 31 years. God waited, then found him in a garden."

Doctor of the Church | Virtue: Faith & Wisdom

The Story

Augustine knew the truth and ran from it anyway.

He grew up in North Africa in the fourth century, the son of a devout Christian mother, Monica, and a pagan father. His mother prayed for him constantly. His father was more interested in Augustine's brilliant mind than his soul. Augustine was, by his own admission, brilliant, restless, and deeply interested in pleasure.

He studied philosophy and rhetoric, became a gifted teacher, and spent years searching for something to believe in. He tried various philosophies and movements, looking for something that could satisfy the hunger he felt but couldn't quite name. None of it worked. He lived with a woman for over a decade and had a son. He moved to Rome, then to Milan. He kept running.

His mother followed him. She prayed without stopping for thirty-one years.

In Milan, Augustine began listening to the bishop Ambrose preach. Something in it reached him. He started reading. He started wrestling. He could feel what he needed to do, and he didn't want to do it. He wrote later, honestly: "Lord, make me chaste, but not yet."

Then one afternoon in a garden, Augustine heard a child's voice singing nearby: "Take up and read." He picked up a letter from Paul. He read a few lines. Something broke open in him.

He was baptized at the age of 32 by St. Ambrose himself. He went home to North Africa, became a priest, then a bishop, and spent the rest of his life writing some of the most important books in the history of Christianity. *His Confessions*, the story of his long detour back to God, is still read today.

Virtue Spotlight: Faith & Wisdom

Faith sometimes looks like a long journey back to something you always knew was true.

Wisdom means learning from your mistakes and letting them make you more honest, not more guarded.

In your life: Is there something you know is right that you've been putting off? Augustine put it off for decades. You don't have to.

Remember This

It's never too late to turn around. God is very good at waiting.

Hero Mission

1. Write down one thing you know you should do that you've been avoiding. Take one step toward it today.

2. Thank someone in your life who has been praying for you or believing in you, even when it seemed impossible.

3. Pray this prayer: *"Lord, my heart is restless until it rests in You."*

Feast Day

August 28 — St. Augustine is one of the greatest theologians in the history of the Church. His mother, St. Monica, has her own feast day on August 27, the day before his, a reminder that her prayers were answered.

CHAPTER 22

St. Patrick

The Enslaved Boy Who Went Back

"He escaped slavery. Then he walked back into that country with the Gospel."

Apostle of Ireland | Virtue: Forgiveness & Zeal

The Story

Patrick was sixteen years old when raiders from Ireland attacked his home in Britain, kidnapped him, and sold him as a slave.

He spent six years working as a shepherd on a cold hillside in Ireland, alone with sheep and wind and silence. He had been raised in a nominally Christian family but hadn't paid much attention to faith. Alone on that hillside, he began to pray. He prayed hundreds of times a day. He prayed in rain and snow. He said later that the Spirit burned in him so strongly that he couldn't stop.

After six years, he heard a voice in a dream telling him his ship was ready. He walked two hundred miles to the coast, found a ship, and eventually made his way home. His family, who thought he was dead, were overjoyed. He was free.

Then he had another dream.

He saw a man from Ireland coming with letters. One was addressed to Patrick. When he read it, he heard the voices of the Irish people crying out: "We beg you, holy boy, come and walk among us again."

Patrick didn't have to go back. He had every reason not to. These were the people who had enslaved him. He went back anyway. He spent years preparing, trained as a priest and bishop, and returned to Ireland as a missionary.

He traveled across the whole island, baptized thousands, ordained priests, established monasteries, and navigated dangerous political terrain with remarkable skill. He faced hostility from pagan chieftains and suspicion from church leaders who doubted him. He kept going. By the time he died, Ireland was largely Christian, and it would go on to become one of the great centers of Christian learning in the medieval world.

Patrick went back not despite what Ireland had done to him, but because he had found something in that suffering worth sharing.

Virtue Spotlight: Forgiveness & Zeal

Forgiveness isn't forgetting. It's choosing not to let what was done to you define what you do next.

Zeal is the fire that keeps you going when the work is long and hard.

In your life: Is there someone who has hurt you that you're still avoiding? You don't have to go back to the same situation, but you can ask God to help you release its hold on you.

Remember This

What was meant to break you can become the very thing that sends you back, stronger.

Hero Mission

1. Think of someone who has hurt you. Pray one prayer for them today, even a short one.

2. Learn one fact about Ireland's Christian history and how it connects to St. Patrick.

3. Pray this prayer: *"Lord, take what was hard in my life and use it for something good."*

Feast Day

March 17 — St. Patrick's Day is celebrated around the world with parades and festivities. At the heart of the celebration is a man who returned to his captors with forgiveness and a message of hope.

NOTES

CHAPTER 23

St. Jerome

The Grumpy Scholar Who Loved God's Word

"He had the worst temper of any saint. He also translated the entire Bible."

Translator of the Bible | Virtue: Wisdom & Fortitude

The Story

Jerome was brilliant, devoted, and famously difficult to get along with.

He was born around 347 in a region now part of Croatia, and from an early age,e it was clear he had an extraordinary mind. He studied in Rome under one of the best teachers of the ancient world, learning Latin, Greek, and eventually Hebrew, which was an almost unheard-of accomplishment for a Christian scholar of his time. He became one of the most learned men alive. He was also impatient, critical, and sharp-tongued with almost everyone he met. His letters are full of arguments. He insulted colleagues. He feuded with other church leaders. He was not, by any reasonable account, easy to be around.

None of that stopped him from doing the most important scholarly work in the history of the Church.

Pope Damasus I asked Jerome to produce a reliable, unified Latin translation of the Bible. The existing translations were inconsistent and full of errors, and the Church needed something trustworthy. Jerome spent years on the project, working from the original Hebrew and Greek texts with extraordinary care. He settled in Bethlehem, surrounded himself with a small community of scholars, and worked through the night by lamplight.

The result was the Vulgate, the Latin Bible that would be the standard text of the Church for over a thousand years. Every Mass said in Latin, every monastery that copied Scripture, every medieval cathedral built on the words of God was drawing on Jerome's work.

He didn't become a saint because he was pleasant. He became a saint because he loved God's Word more than he loved comfort, ease, or the approval of anyone around him.

Virtue Spotlight: Wisdom & Fortitude

Wisdom means pursuing truth seriously, carefully, and with everything you have, even when the work is long.

Fortitude means not giving up on something important just because it's difficult or thankless.

In your life: Do you take your schoolwork seriously? Do you read carefully? Every good habit of learning is a small act in Jerome's tradition.

Remember This

Your worst quality doesn't disqualify you. God uses whole people, flaws and all.

Hero Mission

1. Read one passage from the Bible slowly and carefully today. Look up one word or phrase you don't understand.

2. Think of a subject or skill you've been avoiding because it's hard. Commit to working on it this week.

3. Pray this prayer: *"Lord, give me patience for the long, difficult work*

Feast Day

September 30 — St. Jerome is the patron saint of librarians, translators, and students of Scripture. His image often shows him in a cave with books and a skull, reminders of the solitary, serious work he gave his life to.
that matters most."

CHAPTER 24

St. Brendan the Navigator

The Monk Who Sailed to the Edge of the World

"He launched a leather boat into the North Atlantic. On purpose."

Explorer Saint | Virtue: Faith & Courage

The Story

Brendan was an Irish monk in the sixth century, and one day he decided to sail west into unknown waters to find a place he had heard described as the Land of Promise, a paradise beyond the sea where God's presence was especially close.

He built a boat from wood and animal hides, the traditional

Irish vessel called a currach. He gathered a small crew of monks. And he sailed west into the North Atlantic, one of the most dangerous bodies of water in the world.

What happened over the next seven years, if the accounts are to be believed, was extraordinary. They encountered a column of crystal rising from the sea. They landed on an island that turned out to be a whale. They were attacked by sea creatures and rescued. They found an island where the monks who lived there never aged. They celebrated Easter on the back of a creature so large they thought it was solid ground.

Some of these accounts are clearly symbolic, the traditional language of early medieval adventure stories. But modern historians have noted that Brendan's route, as described, closely mirrors what a skilled sailor could have done in a currach. In 1976, a scholar named Tim Severin built a replica currach and sailed the same route. He made it to Newfoundland.

Whether Brendan reached North America or not, the point of his journey was never geography. It was faith. He set out with a handful of monks, a fragile boat, and a God he trusted completely. He didn't know what was out there. He went anyway.

He came home. He founded monasteries. He kept praying. He died around the year 577 at roughly 93 years old, which is its own kind of miracle.

Virtue Spotlight: Faith & Courage

Faith means acting on trust even when you can't see where you're going.

Courage means getting into the boat anyway.

In your life: Is there something new or uncertain you've been afraid to try? The first step doesn't require certainty. It only requires willingness.

Remember This

You don't need to know the whole route. You just need to trust the One who does.

Hero Mission

1. Try something new this week that feels a little outside your comfort zone.
2. Look at a map and find Ireland, then trace a route across the North Atlantic. Think about what crossing it in a leather boat would have meant.
3. Pray this prayer: *"Lord, give me the courage to go where You lead, even when I can't see the destination."*

Feast Day

May 16 — St. Brendan is the patron saint of sailors, travelers, and explorers. He is one of the most beloved saints in Irish tradition, and his feast is celebrated in coastal communities across Ireland and beyond.

CHAPTER 25

St. Scholastica

The Sister Who Prayed a Storm

"She prayed so hard to keep her brother close that a storm answered."

Sister of St. Benedict | Virtue: Love & Prayer

The Story

Scholastica was Benedict's twin sister, and she had given her life to God just as completely as he had.

She founded and led a community of women near her brother's monastery at Monte Cassino in Italy. They didn't see each other often. Their rule allowed for one visit a year, and even then, they couldn't meet inside the monastery. They would spend the day together in a nearby house, praying, talking, and sharing a meal, and then Benedict would return before nightfall.

One year, as evening approached and Benedict prepared to leave, Scholastica asked him to stay through the night so they could keep talking. Benedict said no. The rule was the rule, and he intended to follow it.

Scholastica folded her hands on the table and prayed.

The sky cracked open. A storm erupted so suddenly and severely that Benedict couldn't go anywhere. He looked at his sister and said, half-exasperated: "What have you done?" She looked back at him calmly and said, "I asked you, and you would not listen, so I asked God, and He did."

They talked through the night. Three days later, from his window, Benedict saw a dove rise into the sky. He understood immediately. Scholastica had died.

She had known it was their last meeting, and she had prayed for one more night. God gave it to her.

What makes Scholastica's story so striking is its directness. She didn't manipulate, plead, or argue. She prayed. She trusted that God heard her. And when God answered, Benedict had nothing to say except to stand in the rain and recognize that his sister's prayer had gone somewhere his rules couldn't follow.

She was buried a few weeks later, and Benedict, when he died, was placed in the same tomb.

Virtue Spotlight: Love & Prayer

Love in Scholastica looked like one more night of conversation, fought for with complete trust in God.

Prayer isn't a last resort. For Scholastica, it was the first and most powerful thing she had.

In your life: When something matters deeply to you, do you pray about it first or last? Scholastica went straight to God.

Remember This

Prayer isn't a backup plan. It's the first and most powerful move you have.

Hero Mission

1. Spend five quiet minutes today telling God something you really want and trusting Him with the answer.
2. Do something kind for a sibling or close friend, something that shows you value time with them.
3. Pray this prayer: *"Lord, teach me to bring everything to You first, before I try to figure it out myself."*

Feast Day

February 10 — St. Scholastica's feast falls just before St. Benedict's on February 10, three days apart, as they died. She is the patron saint of nuns, education, and those who seek protection from storms.

CHAPTER 26

St. Catherine of Alexandria

The Scholar Who Out-argued the Emperor

"She was 18. She debated 50 philosophers – and won."

Patron of Students | Virtue: Wisdom & Courage

The Story

Catherine was eighteen years old, educated, and unafraid.

She came from a noble family in Alexandria, Egypt, one of the great intellectual centers of the ancient world. She had studied philosophy, rhetoric, and theology, and she had converted to Christianity after a vision of Christ. When

Emperor Maxentius began a fierce persecution of Christians around the year 305, Catherine walked into the imperial court and told him to stop.

Maxentius didn't execute her on the spot. He did something he thought was smarter. He gathered fifty of the finest philosophers and scholars in the empire and told them to debate Catherine and destroy her arguments.

She debated all fifty of them. When it was over, the philosophers were convinced, not that Catherine was wrong, but that she was right. Several of them converted to Christianity on the spot. Maxentius had them executed.

He then tried to persuade Catherine by other means. He offered her wealth and a high position at court. She refused. He had her imprisoned and tortured. Christians came to visit her in prison and left as believers. The empress herself visited Catherine and left a Christian. Maxentius had the empress executed,d too. Finally,y he condemned Catherine to be broken on a spiked wheel. According to tradition, the wheel shattered when she touched it. She was executed by beheading around the year 305.

Her story spread across the medieval world,ld and she became one of the most beloved and widely venerated saints in Christian history. She is one of the Fourteen Holy Helpers, a group of saints invoked for particular needs, and she was among the voices Joan of Arc said she heard.

Virtue Spotlight: Wisdom & Courage

Wisdom means knowing what you believe and being able to explain why, clearly and honestly.

Courage means saying what is true in front of people who have the power to punish you for it.

In your life: Do you know what you believe and why? Being able to explain your faith is one of the most valuable things you can develop.

Remember This

A faith you can explain is a faith you can defend. Learn it well.

Hero Mission

1. Pick one thing you believe about God or your faith and look into it more deeply this week.
2. Practice explaining something you believe to a friend or family member in your own words.
3. Pray this prayer: *"Lord, give me a mind that loves truth and a heart that isn't afraid to speak it."*

Feast Day

November 25 — St. Catherine of Alexandria is the patron saint of students, philosophers, teachers, and young women. Many universities in Europe were named in her honor, recognizing her as a model of faithful, courageous learning.

CHAPTER 27

St. Hildegard of Bingen

The Visionary Who Did Everything

"She wrote music, science, theology, and medicine. In the 1100s. As a nun."

Doctor of the Church | Virtue: Wisdom & Zeal

The Story

Hildegard of Bingen was given to the Church at the age of eight.

Her parents, following a practice of the time, entrusted their tenth child to a Benedictine monastery in the German countryside as an offering to God. She grew up inside those walls under the guidance of a woman named Jutta, learned to read Latin and chant the Divine Office, and by all appearances led a quiet, hidden life.

Then, when she was 42,s he started writing everything down.

Hildegard had experienced visions from childhood but had kept them private, afraid of what people would think. Finally, after what she described as a command from God that she could not ignore, she began dictating what she had seen and heard. She called it the "living light." The result was a theological work called Scivias, Know the Ways, a richly detailed account of her visions, which she herself illustrated.

But Hildegard didn't stop at theology. She composed over 70 pieces of music, more than any other composer of the medieval period, and they are still performed and recorded today. She wrote detailed works on natural science and medicine. She described plants, stones, and animals and their uses for healing. She corresponded with popes, emperors, and bishops, offering counsel none of them had asked for but many of them heeded.

She founded her own monastery, fought the local bishop to do it, and won.

She was named a Doctor of the Church in 2012, one of only four women ever to receive that title. When she died in 1179, she was eighty-one years old, and she had been working until the end.

Virtue Spotlight: Wisdom & Zeal

Wisdom in Hildegard meant taking her gifts seriously and trusting that God had given them for a reason.

Zeal means using what you've been given with full commitment, not saving it for later.

In your life: What are you good at? What do you love? Those aren't accidents. They're worth developing and offering.

Remember This

Your gifts are not just for you. They were given to be used.

Hero Mission

1. Make a short list of things you're good at or love to do. Choose one to work on more intentionally this week.

2. Listen to a piece of music composed by Hildegard of Bingen. It is still available and still beautiful.

3. Pray this prayer: *"Lord, show me what You put in me, and help me offer it back to You."*

Feast Day

September 17 — St. Hildegard is the patron saint of musicians, writers, scientists, and those who seek wisdom. Her feast is celebrated with particular joy in Germany, where she spent her entire life and where her music still echoes.

CHAPTER 28

St. Louis IX

The King Who Served at Table

"The most powerful man in Europe spent his afternoons feeding lepers."

King of France | Virtue: Humility & Justice

The Story

Louis IX was the King of France, and by every worldly measure, he had everything.

He came to the throne at twelve years old and ruled for over forty years, presiding over what many historians call the high point of medieval French civilization. He was a skilled administrator, a respected diplomat, and a soldier willing to lead his army into battle personally.

Other European rulers, including his enemies, brought disputes to him for arbitration because they trusted his judgment. He was, by the standards of his time, a genuinely good king.

He was also known to do something that made his courtiers deeply uncomfortable.

Several times a week, Louis would eat with the poor, sometimes with lepers, serving them himself at the table. He funded hospitals, ransomed enslaved Christians, and paid for the care of the blind personally. He kept a mental count of the poor he had fed and made it a daily practice, not an occasion for ceremony. When advisors suggested it was beneath his dignity, he disagreed. He said God would rather judge him for serving the poor than be admired by men for avoiding them.

He led two Crusades. The first ended in his capture and a ruinous ransom. The second, launched when he was already old and unwell, ended in his death from illness in North Africa in 1270. His last words, according to those with him, were about Jerusalem, the city he never reached.

He was canonized just twenty-seven years after his death, one of the fastest canonizations of a king in Church history. He is the only French king ever to be made a saint.

What made Louis remarkable was not his power but how little he used it on himself. He was enormously influential and genuinely humble, a combination that was rare then and remains rare now.

Virtue Spotlight: Humility & Justice

Humility in Louis didn't mean weakness. It meant using power in the service of others rather than for personal glory.

Justice means giving people what they are actually owed, including dignity, care, and a fair hearing. Louis took this seriously in ways that cost him something.

In your life: Is there someone in your life who gets overlooked or treated as less important? Choosing to treat them with full respect is exactly what Louis practiced every day.

Remember This

Power is only worth having if you use it for someone who has none.

Hero Mission

1. Do something today to help someone who cannot repay you. Don't make an occasion of it.
2. Find France on a map and look up what the Crusades were. Think about what it cost Louis to lead them.
3. Pray this prayer: *"Lord, help me use whatever influence I have to serve others, not myself."*

Feast Day

August 25 — St. Louis IX is the patron saint of France, the French monarchy, and the Third Order of St. Francis. Many cities, including St. Louis, Missouri, are named in his honor, a reminder that his example lasted long after his reign.

NOTES

CHAPTER 29

St. Edmund

The King Who Chose Death Over Betrayal

"The Vikings gave him a choice: share your kingdom or die. He refused."

Martyr King | Virtue: Justice & Courage

The Story

Edmund became King of East Anglia in England around t55, when he was only 14 years old.

He ruled for fifteen years and, by all accounts, ruled well. He was known for his fairness, his concern for his people, and his faith, which he took seriously enough to spend a year in prayer and Scripture study early in his reign, learning the Psalms by heart so he could pray them from memory.

In the year 869, the Great Heathen Army of the Vikings, under the command of the Danish leaders Ivar the Boneless and Ubba, invaded East Anglia with a force that had already torn through much of northern England. They were not interested in a negotiated peace.

They offered Edmund a choice. He could share his kingdom, rule jointly under Viking authority, and renounce his Christian faith. Or he could die.

Edmund refused both conditions. He would not abandon his people to Viking rule, nor deny his faith. He was captured, tied to a tree, and used as a target for Viking archers. When he still would not recant, he was beheaded.

He was twenty-nine years old.

Within a generation, he was venerated across England as a martyr. His burial place at Bury St. Edmunds became one of the most visited shrines in medieval England. Kings, pilgrims, and common people came to honor the young king who had chosen death over compromise.

The choice Edmund made was simple, which is not the same as easy. He had a kingdom, a crown, and a future. He gave it all up rather than betray either his people or his God.

Virtue Spotlight: Justice & Courage

Justice means keeping faith with the people who depend on you, even when breaking that faith would save your life.

Courage is not the absence of fear. It is doing what is right, in full knowledge of the cost.

In your life: Have you ever been pressured to go along with something wrong by someone with more power than you?

Edmund's answer was clear and immediate. Deciding in advance what you will and won't do makes that moment easier.

Remember This

A crown is only worth keeping if you can keep it honestly. Edmund knew which one mattered more.

Hero Mission

1. Think of one value you hold that you would not compromise even under pressure. Write it down.

2. Learn where East Anglia is on a map of England and read one fact about the Viking invasions of the ninth century.

3. Pray this prayer: *"Lord, give me the courage to keep my word even when it*

Feast Day

November 20 — St. Edmund is the patron saint of kings, pandemics, and the county of Suffolk in England. His feast was once celebrated as a major holiday across England, and the town of Bury St. Edmunds still bears his name.
costs me something I care about."

NOTES

CHAPTER 30

St. Martin of Tours

The Soldier Who Cut His Cloak in Half

"He split his cloak for a freezing beggar. That night, Christ wore it in his dream."

Patron of Soldiers & France | Virtue: Generosity & Compassion

The Story

Martin was a Roman soldier in the fourth century, the son of a military officer, and he had been enrolled in the army as a teenager, with little say in the matter.

He was stationed in Gaul, which is now France, and by all accounts, he was a decent soldier. But he was also drawn to Christianity in a way that sat uneasily with military life, and he was still a catechumen, studying the faith, not yet baptized.

One winter day, outside the gates of the city of Amiens, Martin encountered a beggar shaking with cold. Martin had no money. He had his military cloak. He drew his sword, cut the cloak in half, and gave half to the beggar.

That night, Martin dreamed that Christ appeared to him wearing the half-cloak. In the dream, Christ said to the angels around him: "Martin, who is not yet baptized, has covered me with this garment." Martin was baptized shortly afterward.

He served in the army for a few more years, but when the emperor Julian ordered him to fight in a battle against Germanic tribes, Martin refused. He told the emperor that he was a soldier of Christ and would not fight. He offered to go to the front lines unarmed as a gesture of his sincerity. He was imprisoned for cowardice. The battle never happened.

Martin eventually left the army, became a monk, then a bishop, and served as the Bishop of Tours for over twenty years. He became one of the most beloved figures in early French Christianity, traveling constantly through his diocese, visiting the poor, challenging the powerful, and living with great simplicity despite his high office.

He died in 397, in a village far from Tours, on a pastoral visit. He had refused to rest until the work was done.

Virtue Spotlight: Generosity & Compassion

Generosity means giving what you actually have, not what is convenient to spare. Martin gave half of something he needed.

Compassion means seeing someone's suffering and responding immediately, without waiting for a better moment.

In your life: The next time you see someone who is cold, hungry, or struggling, what is the first thing you could do? Not a large gesture. Just the first thing.

Remember This

Generosity doesn't wait for the right moment. It acts with what's available right now.

Hero Mission

1. Find something you own that someone else needs more than you do. Give it today.

2. The next time you pass someone who looks cold, tired, or sad, do one concrete thing. Don't just feel bad for them.

3. Pray this prayer: *"Lord, make me quick to give and slow to calculate what it will cost me."*

Feast Day

November 11 — St. Martin's feast, Martinmas, was one of the most widely celebrated holidays in medieval Europe. It is still observed in many countries through lantern processions, feasting, and sharing food with the poor. He is the patron saint of soldiers, beggars, France, and those who work with the poor.

NOTES

CHAPTER 31

St. Joan of Arc

The Peasant Girl Who Led an Army

"She was 17. She heard a voice. She saved France."

Patron of France | Virtue: Courage & Obedience

The Story

oan was a farmer's daughter from a small village in eastern France. She couldn't read or write. She had never held a sword. And in 1429, when France had been losing a war against England for nearly a hundred years, she told the king God had sent her to save the country.

Remarkably, he listened.

The voices had started when Joan

was about thirteen. She heard them while working in her father's garden: St. Michael, St. Catherine, and St. Margaret, she said, speaking to her in light and telling her what to do. For years, she kept it to herself. Then the instructions became too specific to ignore. She was to go to the French king, Charles VII, and help him reclaim his throne.

She walked into his court, identified him despite his attempts to disguise himself among his courtiers, and told him things she could not have known. He gave her a horse, armor, and an army.

At seventeen, Joan rode to the besieged city of Orléans. Within nine days of her arrival, the siege was broken. She went on to lead the French forces in a series of battles that turned the entire war around. Charles was crowned king that same summer, with Joan standing beside him.

A year later, she was captured, sold to the English, and put on trial for heresy. The trial was corrupt from start to finish. She was nineteen years old, defending herself alone, without legal counsel, before trained theologians. She did it with extraordinary clarity. Her responses were so precise that her questioners struggled to find a charge that would hold.

They burned her anyway.

Twenty-five years later, a retrial declared the original verdict unjust. She was canonized in 1920. The girl who had never held a sword became the patron saint of France.

Virtue Spotlight: Courage & Obedience

Courage means acting on what you know is right, even when no one around you believes it's possible.

Obedience means trusting God's direction even when it leads somewhere frightening and strange.

In your life: Has God, a parent, or a trusted adult ever asked you to do something that felt too big for you? That feeling is normal. It didn't stop Joan.

Remember This

God doesn't always call the qualified. He qualifies the call.

Hero Mission

1. Do one thing today that feels slightly too big for you. Start anyway.
2. Learn one fact about the Hundred Years' War and where Joan fits into it.
3. Pray this prayer: "Lord, when You call me to something hard, give me the courage to take the first step."

Feast Day

May 30 — St. Joan of Arc is the patron saint of France and soldiers. Her feast is celebrated with particular pride in France, where she is as much a national hero as a saint.

CHAPTER 32

St. Elizabeth of Hungary

The Princess Who Gave Everything Away

"She was a princess. She spent her fortune on hospitals and starving people."

Patron of the Poor | Virtue: Generosity & Charity

The Story

Elizabeth was four years old when she arrived at the castle in Thuringia, Germany, sent there as a future bride for the young landgrave Ludwig. She grew up inside those walls, surrounded by wealth, attended by servants, and given everything a princess could want.

She gave most of it away.

From childhood, Elizabeth was drawn to the poor in a way that made her household uneasy. She would sneak food from the castle to people in the town below. She gave away her own possessions. The courtiers around her found it embarrassing. Her mother-in-law found it troubling. Elizabeth kept going.

When she married Ludwig at fourteen, she found in him a rare thing: a husband who supported her. He didn't try to stop her charity. He protected it. When she built a hospital at the foot of the castle hill and spent her days personally caring for the sick, washing patients, and sitting with the dying, he let her.

Then Ludwig died of plague on his way to the Crusades. Elizabeth was twenty years old, pregnant with her third child, and suddenly without protection.

Her brother-in-law expelled her from the castle. She gave birth in a barn on the coldest night of the year, found shelter where she could, and refused to return, even when offered her position back. Instead, she gave away the last of her inheritance, joined the Third Order of St. Francis, and spent the remaining years of her short life running a hospital in the town of Marburg.

She died at twenty-four. She had been a princess. She chose to die as a servant of the poor.

The Church canonized her just four years after her death, one of the fastest canonizations in history.

Virtue Spotlight: Generosity & Charity

Generosity means giving not from your surplus but from what actually costs you something.

Charity is love in action. Elizabeth didn't send money. She showed up.

In your life: Is there someone around you who needs not just things but presence? Sometimes the most generous gift is your time and attention.

Remember This

Real generosity costs something. That's what makes it real.

Hero Mission

1. Give something away today that you actually like, not something you were planning to throw out.
2. Find out if there is a food pantry, shelter, or service organization near you. Learn what they need.
3. Pray this prayer: *"Lord, open my eyes to the people around me who need more than I've been giving."*

Feast Day

November 17 — St. Elizabeth of Hungary is the patron saint of the poor, hospitals, bakers, and those who perform charitable work. Many Catholic hospitals and charities around the world bear her name.

NOTES

CHAPTER 33

St. Francis of Assisi

The Friend of All Creation

"He gave everything back to his father and walked out smiling."

Patron of Animals & Ecology | Virtue: Generosity & Joy

The Story

Francis was the son of a wealthy cloth merchant in Assisi, Italy, and for the first part of his life, he lived like it. He wore fine clothes, spent freely, threw parties, and dreamed of becoming a knight. He was charming, popular, and going nowhere in particular.

Then a series of things happened that he couldn't shake.

He was captured in a small war and spent a year in prison. He came home sick. During a long recovery, he began to feel that the life he had been living was hollow. He started praying in ruined chapels outside the city. One day, he said, he heard Christ speak to him from a crucifix: "Francis, rebuild my Church."

He took it literally at first and began restoring old chapels stone by stone. He also did something that shocked everyone who knew him: he embraced a leper on the road. Francis had always been terrified of lepers. He didn't know what made him stop. He said afterward that what had seemed bitter became sweet.

The confrontation with his father came next. Francis had been selling cloth from the family warehouse to fund his rebuilding work. His father dragged him before the bishop to demand the money back. Francis returned every coin, then took off his expensive clothes and handed those back, too, standing in the square in front of the whole town. He walked away with nothing and never looked back.

He gathered followers. He wrote a simple rule: own nothing, preach everywhere, serve the poor, love all creatures. The Franciscan order he founded became one of the largest and most influential in the history of the Church. He preached to birds. He wrote a poem praising Brother Sun and Sister Moon. He died on the ground because he wanted to meet death the same way he had met everything else, with empty hands and a full heart.

Virtue Spotlight: Generosity & Joy

Generosity in Francis was total. He didn't give from his surplus. He gave until there was nothing left, and called it freedom.

Joy was the result. Francis is one of the happiest figures in the history of Christianity, and his happiness came directly from letting go.

In your life: Is there something you're holding onto too tightly? Loosening your grip on things is the beginning of Francis's kind of freedom.

Remember This

The less you cling to, the more room you have for what actually matters.

Hero Mission

1. Give away something you've been keeping that someone else could use more.
2. Spend five minutes outside today and pay attention to one thing in nature you normally walk past.
3. Pray this prayer: *"Lord, make me an instrument of Your peace."*

Feast Day

October 4 — St. Francis's feast is celebrated around the world with the Blessing of the Animals, when people bring their pets and working animals to church. He is the patron saint of animals, ecology, and Italy.

NOTES

CHAPTER 34

St. Dominic

The Preacher Who Fought Heresy with Truth

"While everyone else wanted force, Dominic grabbed a book and started talking."

Founder of the Dominicans | Virtue: Zeal & Wisdom

The Story

In the early 1200s, a movement called Catharism had spread across southern France and was pulling people away from the Church in large numbers. The Cathars taught that the physical world was evil, rejected the sacraments, and denied the resurrection. Church leaders were alarmed. Some called for military force.

Dominic had a different idea.

He had traveled through the region and noticed something: the Cathar preachers were impressive. They walked everywhere, owned nothing, lived simply, and talked to people. The Catholic priests sent to oppose them often arrived on horseback with an entourage, stayed in comfortable lodgings, and left quickly. No one was persuaded.

Dominic began preaching on foot, without money, sleeping where he could, and engaging the Cathars in direct debate. He argued clearly, patiently, and with genuine learning. He founded the Order of Preachers, a community of preachers built on study, poverty, and preaching, now known as the Dominicans.

The rule of his order was unusual: every house was to have a library, every friar was to study seriously, and no one was to preach without preparation. Dominic understood that bad ideas are best answered with better ones, explained clearly by people who have actually thought them through.

He also prayed constantly. Witnesses who traveled with him described him praying through the night in churches along the road. He is credited with spreading devotion to the Rosary, the repetitive, meditative prayer that became one of the most widely practiced forms of Catholic prayer in the world.

Dominic died in 1221, exhausted, having given everything to his mission. He was canonized nine years later.

Virtue Spotlight: Zeal & Wisdom

Zeal means caring about something so much that you organize your whole life around it. Dominic built an entire order around the conviction that truth, clearly spoken, could change minds.

Wisdom means knowing that the right approach matters as much as the right answer.

In your life: When you disagree with someone, do you listen first? Understanding someone else's position before you respond is a skill worth building.

Remember This

The best answer to a bad idea is a better idea, explained well and lived honestly.

Hero Mission

1. The next time you disagree with someone, listen to their full argument before responding.

2. Learn what the Rosary is and try praying one decade.

3. Pray this prayer: *"Lord, give me wisdom to understand and courage to speak the truth clearly."*

Feast Day

August 8 — St. Dominic is the patron saint of astronomers, the Dominican Republic, and those who preach the faith. His order has produced some of the greatest theologians and teachers in the history of the Church.

CHAPTER 35

St. Thomas Aquinas

The Silent Ox Who Shook the World

"His classmates called him the Dumb Ox. He became the greatest theologian in history."

Doctor of the Church | Virtue: Wisdom & Humility

The Story

Thomas was a large, quiet boy, and his fellow students at the University of Naples assumed he was slow.

He wasn't slow. He was thinking.

He came from a noble family in southern Italy, and they had ambitious plans for him: he would become the abbot of Monte Cassino, Benedict's famous monastery, a position of considerable power and prestige. Thomas had other plans. He wanted to join the newly founded Dominican order, the wandering preachers who owned nothing and studied everything. His family was horrified. His brothers kidnapped him and locked him in the family castle for over a year, trying to change his mind.

He spent the year studying.

When he finally joined the Dominicans, he came under the guidance of the great scholar Albertus Magnus, who recognized immediately what no one else had seen. When other students mocked Thomas for his silence, Albertus told them: "You call him the Dumb Ox, but one day the bellowing of this ox will resound throughout the whole world."

Thomas spent his life doing one thing: thinking carefully about God, faith, and reason, and writing it down. His masterwork, the *Summa Theologica,* is an attempt to answer every major question about the faith, systematically and with complete intellectual honesty. It runs to millions of words. It is still used in seminaries today.

Near the end of his life, while praying, Thomas had an experience that left him unable to write another word. When pressed to continue, he said simply: "All that I have written seems to me like straw compared to what I have seen."

He died at forty-nine, on his way to a Church council, stopping to rest at a monastery. He never finished the *Summa.*

Virtue Spotlight: Wisdom & Humility

Wisdom means thinking seriously about what matters most and not settling for easy answers.

Humility means knowing that everything you've learned is still just the beginning.

In your life: Do you take your studies seriously? Every subject you learn well prepares you to understand more of the world God made.

Remember This

The more you truly learn, the more you realize how much is left to discover.

Hero Mission

1. Pick a question about your faith you've never thought through carefully. Write it down and look for an answer.
2. The next time someone dismisses you or underestimates you, let your work speak instead of your words.
3. Pray this prayer: *"Lord, give me a humble mind that loves truth more than being right."*

Feast Day

January 28 — St. Thomas Aquinas is the patron saint of students, scholars, universities, and theologians. His feast is celebrated in Catholic schools around the world.

NOTES

CHAPTER 36

St. Ignatius of Loyola

The Soldier God Stopped with a Cannonball

"A cannonball shattered his legs. It gave him two months to think. That was enough."

Founder of the Jesuits | Virtue: Prudence & Zeal

The Story

Ignatius wanted to be a hero. He just had the wrong idea of what heroism looked like.

He was a Spanish nobleman, trained as a soldier, ambitious and vain, fond of fine clothes and dueling and the company of women. In 1521, during the defense of the city of Pamplona against a French army, a cannonball struck him and shattered both his legs. The battle was over. Ignatius was carried back to the family castle to recover

.

The recovery took months, and there was almost nothing to do. He asked for books about knights and romance, his usual reading. None were available. He was given a life of Christ and a collection of stories about the saints.

He read them. Then he read them again.

He began to notice something. When he imagined his old life, the battles and glory and romance, he felt a brief excitement that always faded into restlessness. When he imagined living as the saints had, he felt something different: a quiet joy that stayed. He started paying attention to that difference.

After his recovery, Ignatius undertook a long pilgrimage, spent nearly a year in a cave in prayer, and eventually went back to school. He was in his thirties, sitting in classes with teenagers, learning Latin from the beginning. He spent 11 years studying before founding the Society of Jesus, the Jesuits, in 1540.

The order he built was unlike anything before it: rigorously educated, highly disciplined, and sent everywhere. Jesuits taught in universities, worked as missionaries in Asia and the Americas, and advised kings. The cannonball that ended Ignatius's first career launched a second one that changed the world.

Virtue Spotlight: Prudence & Zeal

Prudence means paying attention to what your inner life is telling you and being honest about it. Ignatius built an entire method of prayer around that practice.

Zeal means throwing everything you have into what you know is right, once you've figured out what that is.

In your life: Pay attention this week to what brings you lasting peace versus what excites you briefly and leaves you empty. That difference matters.

Remember This

Not all excitement is the same. Learn to tell the difference between what fills you and what just distracts you.

Hero Mission

1. At the end of today, ask yourself: what made me feel genuinely peaceful? What just passed through?

2. Learn what the Jesuits do and find one school, hospital, or mission they founded near where you live.

3. Pray this prayer: *"Lord, show me the difference between what I want and what I truly need."*

Feast Day

July 31 — St. Ignatius of Loyola is the patron saint of soldiers, educators, and the Jesuit order. Jesuit schools around the world mark his feast with particular celebration.

NOTES

CHAPTER 37

St. Francis Xavier

The Man Who Never Stopped Sailing

"In 11 years, he covered India, Japan, and the edge of China."

Patron of Missions | Virtue: Zeal & Fortitude

The Story

Francis Xavier was one of the original seven men who, with Ignatius of Loyola, founded the Jesuits in Paris. He was brilliant, charming, and athletic, exactly the kind of person who could have had a comfortable career in a European university. He chose the opposite.

In 1541, the King of Portugal asked for missionaries to be sent to his territories in Asia. Ignatius chose

Francis. He sailed from Lisbon and arrived in Goa, on the western coast of India, after a brutal thirteen-month voyage. He immediately went to work.

Over the next eleven years, he never stopped. He worked along the coast of India, baptizing thousands, visiting the sick and the imprisoned, and learning enough of the local language to teach basic prayers. He sailed to the islands of Southeast Asia. He traveled to Japan, learned Japanese well enough to preach, and established the first Christian community there. He wrote letters back to Europe that inspired a generation of young men to join the missions.

He never used interpreters when he could avoid it. He learned the languages himself. He slept on the ground. He ate what was available. Witnesses said he had an energy and joy about him that people found irresistible.

By 1552, he had set his sights on China, which was closed to foreigners. He made it to a small island just off the Chinese coast, within sight of the mainland, and waited for a way in. No passage came. He fell ill on the island and died there, alone except for a young Chinese convert who stayed with him. He was forty-six years old.

In eleven years, Francis Xavier had traveled further than almost any missionary in history and baptized more people than any individual since the apostles.

Virtue Spotlight: Zeal & Fortitude

Zeal is what gets you onto the ship. It's caring about the mission more than your own comfort.

Fortitude is what keeps you going when the voyage is long, the language is hard, and the work is slow.

In your life: Is there something you believe in enough to be inconvenienced for it? That inconvenience is where real commitment begins.

Remember This

The work worth doing is rarely comfortable. That's not a reason to stop. It's usually a sign you're going the right direction.

Hero Mission

1. Find Goa, Japan, and the island of Shangchuan on a map—Trace Francis Xavier's route.

2. Think of one thing you've been putting off because it seemed too hard. Take one concrete step today.

3. Pray this prayer: *"Lord, give me the zeal to go where You send me and the fortitude to stay."*

Feast Day

December 3 — St. Francis Xavier is the patron saint of missionaries, foreign missions, and many countries in Asia. He is one of the most widely venerated saints in the Catholic Church worldwide.

CHAPTER 38

St. Clare of Assisi

The Girl Who Followed Francis

"She ran away from home at midnight to follow God. Her family chased her. She held the altar and wouldn't let go."

Founder of the Poor Clares | Virtue: Courage & Poverty

The Story

Clare was eighteen years old when she heard Francis of Assisi preach, and she understood immediately that he was describing something she had already been longing for.

She came from one of the noble families of Assisi. Her future was arranged: a suitable husband, a comfortable household, the kind of life her family had built. Clare wanted none of it. She had been quietly giving food and money to people experiencing poverty for years, against her family's wishes. What Francis described, a life of radical poverty and complete devotion to God, made sense to her in a way nothing else had.

On the night of Palm Sunday, 1212, Clare slipped out of her family home in the dark and walked through the woods to meet Francis and his brothers. They received her, cut her hair as a sign of her consecration to God, and placed her in a nearby Benedictine convent for safety.

Her family came to take her back. She held onto the altar and refused to move. Her family came again. She held on again. Eventually, they stopped coming.

Clare founded a community of women at San Damiano, the little chapel Francis had rebuilt with his own hands years before. She called them the Poor Ladies. They owned nothing, neither as individuals nor as a community. She had to fight the Church's own authorities for years to be allowed to keep that poverty, because no religious community for women had ever lived that way before. She won.

She governed San Damiano for over forty years. She never left. From that small enclosure, she shaped the lives of thousands and exchanged letters with popes and queens. She died in 1253, the founding document of her order finally approved, in her hands.

Virtue Spotlight: Courage & Poverty

Courage meant letting go of everything her family had built and holding onto the altar when they came to pull her away.

Poverty in Clare wasn't deprivation. It was freedom, the freedom to belong entirely to God.

In your life: Is there something you're holding onto that keeps you from something better? Sometimes the bravest thing is letting go.

Remember This

Holding on and letting go both take courage. The question is knowing which one God is asking for.

Hero Mission

1. Identify one possession or habit you're overly attached to. Ask God what He thinks about it.

2. Do something quietly generous today without expecting anything in return.

3. Pray this prayer: *"Lord, help me hold onto You more tightly than anything else."*

Feast Day

August 11 — St. Clare is the patron saint of television, eye disease, embroiderers, and those who follow the contemplative life. The Poor Clares, the order she founded, continue their life of prayer in communities around the world today.

CHAPTER 39

St. Teresa of Ávila

The Doctor Who Argued with God

"She had a temper, a sense of humor, and reformed an entire religious order."

Doctor of the Church | Virtue: Wisdom & Courage

The Story

Teresa of Ávila was not what most people picture when they think of a saint.

She was funny. She was sharp-tongued. She had a temper and knew it. She enjoyed conversation, was fond of good food, and once complained to God after a particularly difficult journey: "If this is how You treat Your friends, it's no wonder You have so few." She wrote that down and kept it.

She entered a Carmelite convent in Spain at twenty years old. For nearly twenty years, she drifted, distracted, more comfortable with the active social life of the convent's parlor than with deep prayer. She was not a fraud, exactly, but she wasn't fully present either.

Then, in her early forties, she looked at an image of the wounded Christ and something broke open. She began to pray in earnest and entered what she would later describe as the deepest possible relationship with God, a series of experiences so real and consuming that she struggled to find language for them. She wrote two of the most important books about prayer ever written: her autobiography and The Interior Castle, a detailed map of the soul's journey toward God.

She also reformed her entire religious order. The Carmelite convents of her day had become comfortable and unfocused. Teresa founded a new, stricter branch and spent years traveling across Spain on difficult roads, in poor health, arguing with Church authorities and local officials, founding convent after convent until she had established seventeen new houses.

She died in 1582, on the road, returning from yet another foundation. She was sixty-seven. She was named a Doctor of the Church in 1970, one of only four women ever to receive that title.

Virtue Spotlight: Wisdom & Courage

Wisdom in Teresa came from honest prayer: she knew herself clearly, and she knew God even better.

Courage meant reforming what was broken,n even when powerful people wanted her to stop.

In your life: Are you honest in your prayer, or do you tell God what you think He wants to hear? Teresa was always honest. It made all the difference.

Remember This

God can handle your honesty. He already knows what you're thinking.

Hero Mission

1. Spend five minutes in honest prayer today. Say what you actually feel, not what you think you should say.
2. Think of one thing in your life that has become comfortable but isn't really helping you grow. Talk to God about it.
3. Pray this prayer: *"Lord, take me deeper than comfort and closer than I've dared to go before."*

Feast Day

October 15 — St. Teresa of Ávila is the patron saint of headache sufferers, Spain, and those who seek a deep life of prayer. Her feast is celebrated with joy in Carmelite communities around the world.

CHAPTER 40

St. Rose of Lima

The First Saint of the Americas

"She was the most famous person in Lima. She hid in a garden shed to be closer to God."

Patron of Latin America | Virtue: Penance & Charity

The Story

Rose was born in Lima, Peru, in 1586, and she was beautiful. Everyone said so. Her mother was proud of it. Her neighbors admired it. And Rose, for reasons that were hard to explain to anyone around her, found it more of a burden than a gift.

She wasn't ungrateful or dramatic about it. She simply noticed that her appearance drew a kind of attention that made it harder to focus on what she actually cared about. She cut her hair. She rubbed pepper on her face. She wanted people to see past the surface to something she thought mattered more.

What she cared about was God and the poor.

She had been deeply devout from childhood, taking St. Catherine of Siena as her model. At fifteen, she received the Dominican habit, becoming a member of the Third Order of St. Dominic while continuing to live at home. She built a small hermitage in the garden and spent long hours there in prayer, sometimes through the night. She also brought the sick and the dying into her home to care for them, beginning what is sometimes called the first social welfare institution in the Americas.

Her prayer life was intense. She described periods of profound consolation and periods of complete spiritual darkness, years in which she felt nothing, when prayer felt like speaking into silence. She kept going.

When she died in 1617 at the age of thirty-one, the city of Lima was overwhelmed with grief. Crowds lined the streets for her funeral. Government officials served as her pallbearers. Twelve years later, she became the first person born in the Americas to be canonized by the Church.

Virtue Spotlight: Penance & Charity

Penance doesn't mean punishing yourself. It means taking your inner life seriously enough to discipline it with intention.

Charity is love made concrete. Rose didn't just pray

for the poor. She brought them inside.

In your life: Is there one distraction in your life you could quietly remove to make more room for what matters? Start small.

Remember This

Fame and attention are not the same as a life well lived. Rose knew the difference.

Hero Mission

1. Identify one thing that distracts you from prayer or quiet. Set it aside for one hour today.

2. Do something for someone who is sick or struggling, something that requires actual effort.

3. Pray this prayer: *"Lord, help me want the right things, and let go of the rest."*

Feast Day

August 23 — St. Rose of Lima is the patron saint of Latin America, the Philippines, and those who suffer ridicule for their piety. Her feast is celebrated with particular devotion in Peru, where she remains a beloved national saint.

CHAPTER 41

St. Thomas More

The Man Who Kept His Word to God

"The king offered him everything. He said no – and made a joke on the scaffold."

Patron of Lawyers & Statesmen | Virtue: Justice & Fortitude

The Story

Thomas More was the most powerful lawyer in England, and King Henry VIII trusted him completely.

More was brilliant, witty, and deeply principled. He served as Henry's Lord Chancellor, the highest legal office in the kingdom, and was known throughout Europe for his learning and integrity. He had written books, raised a family he adored, and built a life most men would have envied.

Then Henry VIII decided he wanted a divorce. The Pope said no. Henry decided to make himself head of the Church of England instead, cutting ties with Rome entirely. He asked his advisors, his bishops, and his court to sign an oath acknowledging him as the supreme head of the Church and the legitimacy of his new marriage.
Almost everyone signed.

More refused. He didn't make a speech about it. He didn't organize a protest. He simply declined quietly and withdrew from public life. Henry had him imprisoned in the Tower of London. For over a year, More sat in a cold cell while friends, family members, and the king's agents came to persuade him to change his mind. His own daughter begged him.

He told her he loved her too much to give her a father who had lost his soul.

At his trial, More was convicted based on perjured testimony. He was sentenced to death. On the scaffold, he helped the executioner steady the block, asked for a moment to move his beard out of the way, and remarked that it, at least, had committed no treason. Then he lay his head down.

He was executed on July 6, 1535. Four hundred years later, the Church canonized him. He is the patron saint of lawyers, politicians, and anyone who has ever been asked to sign something they knew was wrong.

Virtue Spotlight: Justice & Fortitude

Justice means doing what is right regardless of who is asking you to do otherwise.

Fortitude means holding your ground when everything around you is giving way.

In your life: Has anyone ever pressured you to go along with something you knew was wrong? Saying no politely but firmly is exactly what More did.

Remember This

A person's word to God is the one promise no king can dissolve.

Hero Mission

1. Think of one situation where you've been pressured to go along with something wrong. Decide now what you'll say next time.

2. Learn what the phrase "man for all seasons" means and why it was applied to Thomas More.

3. Pray this prayer: *"Lord, give me the courage to do what is right even when everyone around me is doing otherwise."*

Feast Day

June 22 — St. Thomas More is celebrated together with St. John Fisher, his fellow martyr. He is the patron saint of lawyers, statesmen, and those who work in public life, a reminder that integrity and power can coexist.

CHAPTER 42

St. John Fisher

The Last Bishop Standing

"Every bishop in England signed the oath. Everyone except John Fisher."

Bishop & Martyr | Virtue: Fortitude & Courage

The Story

John Fisher was an older man when they came for him, and he had been expecting it.

He had served as the Bishop of Rochester for over thirty years, one of the most respected churchmen in England. He was a scholar, a friend of Erasmus and Thomas More, and known for the simplicity of his life despite holding high office. He kept a skull on his dining table as a reminder that life is short and what matters is what comes after.

When Henry VIII began his campaign to annul his marriage to Catherine of Aragon and break with Rome, Fisher was one of the few voices willing to say openly that the king was wrong. He wrote pamphlets, argued in Parliament, and refused to be quiet. Henry tolerated it for a time. Fisher was old, his health was poor, and perhaps the king hoped he would simply stop.

He didn't stop.

When the Act of Supremacy was passed, requiring every bishop in England to take an oath acknowledging Henry as the head of the Church, Fisher refused. Every other bishop in England signed. Some signed reluctantly. Some signed with reservations they kept to themselves. Fisher simply said no.

He was imprisoned in the Tower of London. His cell was cold. He was given little food. His health deteriorated badly. When Pope Paul III made Fisher a cardinal in an attempt to pressure Henry into releasing him, Henry reportedly said that Fisher would have no head to put the hat on by the time it arrived.

He was right. Fisher was executed on June 22, 1535, two weeks before Thomas More. He was nearly eighty years old.

At his execution, witnesses noted that he was so weak he could barely climb the scaffold. Once he was on it, he stood upright, quoted Scripture, and died with a clarity that moved everyone watching.

He had spent his whole life preparing for exactly this.

Virtue Spotlight: Fortitude & Courage

Fortitude is what remains when every external support is removed. Fisher had nothing left except his conscience, and he held it.

Courage in an older man with failing health, standing completely alone, is one of the most striking examples in this book.
In your life: Have you ever been the only person in a room who held a particular view? That loneliness is real, and enduring it with dignity takes genuine strength.

Remember This

Being the last one standing for something true is not failure. It is the clearest kind of success.

Hero Mission

1. Think about something you believe that the people around you don't share. How would you explain it clearly and calmly?
2. Look up what a cardinal's hat looks like. Remember what Henry said, and what Fisher chose instead.
3. Pray this prayer: *"Lord, help me stand for what is right even when I am standing alone."*

Feast Day

June 22 — St. John Fisher is celebrated together with St. Thomas More. He is a patron of those who work in education and bishops, a reminder that learning and faithfulness belong together.

NOTES

CHAPTER 43

St. Nicholas Owen

The Builder Who Hid Priests in the Walls

"He built secret rooms in houses for 26 years. He was never betrayed."

Carpenter Martyr | Virtue: Charity & Prudence

The Story

Nicholas Owen was a small man who did quiet work that saved hundreds of lives.

In Elizabethan England, being a Catholic priest was a capital offense. Practicing the Catholic faith was dangerous. Priests moved in secret from house to house, saying Mass in back rooms and attics, always at risk of arrest. When a house was raided, which happened often, the question was simple: where had the priest gone?

That was Nicholas Owen's specialty.

He was a carpenter and a lay brother in the Jesuit order. For twenty-six years, he traveled across England, entering the homes of Catholic families, and building hiding places so perfect that priest-hunters could search a house for days and find nothing. He built rooms inside chimneys, below floors, behind false walls, and inside staircases. He worked alone and at night, so that even the families he helped often didn't know the full details of what he had built. If they were arrested and interrogated, they couldn't reveal what they didn't know.

The hiding places he built are called priest holes, and many of them still exist today, discovered centuries later in old English manor houses. Some are barely large enough to sit in. Priests would hide in them for days at a time, in complete silence, while pursuivants knocked on the walls searching for hollow spaces.

Owen was eventually captured in 1606, after hiding with two priests during a raid on Hindlip Hall. The researchers had spent eleven days going through the house before he surrendered voluntarily, emerging to distract the searchers and give his companions more time.

He was tortured severely and died in the Tower of London in 1606. He had never given a single name.

Virtue Spotlight: Charity & Prudence

Charity means putting yourself at risk so that someone else doesn't have to. Owen's entire life was built around the safety of others.

Prudence means thinking carefully so that the good you're trying to do actually works. Owen was meticulous precisely because sloppiness would have gotten people killed.

In your life: Is there someone you could help in a quiet, practical way that doesn't require any recognition? That kind of service is exactly what Owen modeled.

Remember This

The most important work is often invisible. The people doing it rarely get credit. That's the point.

Hero Mission

1. Do something helpful for someone today without telling anyone.
2. Learn what a priest hole looks like. Search "Harvington Hall priest holes" and see how small they are.
3. Pray this prayer: *"Lord, help me serve others in hidden ways, without needing anyone to notice."*

Feast Day

October 25 — St. Nicholas Owen is celebrated as part of the group known as the Forty Martyrs of England and Wales, canonized in 1970 by Pope Paul VI. He is the patron saint of those who do work that never gets public recognition.

CHAPTER 44

St. Isaac Jogues

The Missionary Who Came Back with Broken Hands

"They cut off his fingers and sent him home. He asked to go back.""

Martyr of North America | Virtue: Fortitude & Charity

The Story

Isaac Jogues was a French Jesuit priest who came to North America in 1636 to work as a missionary among the Huron people in what is now Canada. He learned the language, lived among the Huron, and devoted himself to his mission with everything he had.

In 1642, while traveling by canoe, his group was ambushed by a Mohawk raiding party. Jogues and his companions were captured, beaten, and marched to a Mohawk village. What followed was months of brutal captivity. The Mohawks cut off most of his fingers. They burned him, forced him to run gauntlets, and tortured his companions while he watched.

Jogues survived. He was eventually smuggled out of captivity with the help of Dutch traders and made his way back to France. The damage to his hands was permanent. He could no longer hold a chalice properly at Mass. He wrote to Rome and asked for permission to celebrate Mass despite his injuries. The Pope granted it, reportedly saying that it would be a shame to prevent a martyr of Christ from offering the sacrifice of Christ.

Then Jogues asked to go back.

He returned to North America in 1644, not to the Huron mission this time but on a diplomatic mission to the Mohawk. He went back knowing exactly what might happen. He carried a small box of belongings, which the Mohawks later blamed for a subsequent crop failure and an outbreak of disease. He was seized, condemned, and killed with a tomahawk on October 18, 1646.

He had known the risk before he went. He went because the mission mattered more than his safety.

Virtue Spotlight: Fortitude & Charity

Fortitude means enduring severe suffering without abandoning what you came to do. Jogues endured more than most people could imagine and went back for more.

Charity means loving people enough to return to them even when they've hurt you.

In your life, has anyone ever hurt you and then needed your help? Choosing to help anyway is one of the hardest things a person can do. Jogues did it with his whole life.

Remember This

The measure of love is not what it costs you to give it. It's whether you give it anyway.

Hero Mission

1. Think of someone unkind to you. Ask God to help you wish them well today.
2. Find North America on a map and locate the region of the Huron and Mohawk nations. Think about what it meant to travel there in 1636.
3. Pray this prayer: *"Lord, give me a love that doesn't stop at the limits of what's comfortable."*

Feast Day

October 19 — St. Isaac Jogues is celebrated with the other North American Martyrs, a group of Jesuits who died in New France in the 17th century. He is the patron saint of Canada and the Americas.

CHAPTER 45

St. John Bosco

The Priest Who Juggled for Jesus

"He taught himself juggling as a boy to draw crowds – then catechized them."

Patron of Youth | Virtue: Charity & Zeal

The Story

John Bosco grew up poor in rural Italy in the early 1800s, and he figured out early that if you wanted to reach people, you had to meet them where they were.

As a boy, he taught himself juggling, acrobatics, and card tricks so he could gather the village children around him. Once he had a crowd, he would retell the Sunday sermon and lead them in prayer. By the time he was ordained a priest in 1841, he had spent years thinking about how to reach young people, and he had some clear ideas.

Turin, the city where he worked, was full of boys in trouble. Boys who had come from the countryside looking for work, boys who had ended up in prison, boys with no education and no one looking out for them. Don Bosco, as he was known, started gathering them. He found rooms, then buildings. He offered schools, workshops, and apprenticeships. He also offered football, theater, music, and laughter, because he understood that a boy who is having fun is a boy who is staying out of worse situations.

His method was simple but unusual for his time. He refused to use fear or punishment as his primary tools. Instead, he built relationships. He walked among his boys in the yard during recreation, talked to them, knew them by name, and treated them with dignity. He called it the Preventive System: prevent problems by being present, not by punishing after the fact.

He founded the Salesians, a religious order dedicated to the education and care of young people, which grew to become one of the largest religious orders in the world. He died in 1888 at sixty-two, having founded schools, trade centers, and missions across three continents.

The morning after he died, thousands of young people lined the streets to say goodbye.

Virtue Spotlight: Charity & Zeal

Charity in Don Bosco meant showing up for people the world had written off, again and again, without growing tired of it.

Zeal means bringing energy and creativity to the work, not going through the motions.

In your life: Is there someone in your school or neighborhood who gets overlooked? Notice them this week. That's exactly the kind of attention Don Bosco gave.

Remember This

The best way to reach someone is actually to like them. Don Bosco genuinely liked his boys, and they knew it.

Hero Mission

1. Learn one simple skill you could use to make someone laugh or smile today. Use it.
2. Think of one person in your life who feels overlooked. Do one concrete thing to let them know you see them.
3. Pray this prayer: *"Lord, give me the creativity and energy to reach the people around me where they actually are."*

Feast Day

January 31 — St. John Bosco is the patron saint of youth, students, apprentices, and editors. Salesian schools and youth centers operate in over 130 countries today, continuing the work he began in a small rented room in Turin.

CHAPTER 46

St. John Vianney

The Priest They Tried to Drive Away

"He was sent to the worst parish in France. People came from all over Europe."

Patron of Priests | Virtue: Charity & Perseverance

The Story

John Vianney almost didn't become a priest.

He was a slow student who struggled with Latin, and the seminary examined him twice and nearly turned him away. His professors finally agreed to ordain him on one condition: they would send him somewhere no one else wanted to go. In 1818, he was assigned to Ars, a tiny village in rural France that hadn't had a functioning parish in years and where, by most accounts, the faith had gone cold.

He arrived on foot, got lost in the dark, and asked a young shepherd for directions. The boy pointed him toward Ars. Vianney told him, "You have shown me the way to Ars. I will show you the way to heaven."

He was there for forty-one years.

At first, nothing much happened. He preached, visited the sick, and worked to restore the church building. He slept very little and ate almost nothing. Slowly, things began to change. The taverns and the Sunday dances, which had been the main entertainment in the village, began losing their pull. People started going to Mass. Then people from neighboring villages started coming. Then people from across France.

Within a decade, Ars had become one of the most visited places in the country. People came to confess to Vianney, sometimes waiting for days in lines that stretched outside the church. He would spend sixteen or eighteen hours a day in the confessional. He could, witnesses said, tell people things about themselves he had no natural way of knowing.

He asked three times to be relieved and allowed to go live as a simple monk somewhere. Each time the bishop said no.

He died in 1859. Thousands attended his funeral.

Virtue Spotlight: Charity & Perseverance

Charity meant showing up for his parish every single day for forty-one years, with no fanfare and no reward except the work itself.

Perseverance means doing the right thing long after the excitement of starting has worn off.

In your life: Is there something you've been doing faithfully for a long time with no visible results? That faithfulness is exactly what Vianney practiced, and it changed a village.

Remember This

Showing up every day, even when nothing seems to be happening, is its own form of heroism.

Hero Mission

1. Choose one good habit and commit to doing it every day for one week, even on the days you don't feel like it.

2. If you're Catholic, consider going to confession this month. Think about what Vianney gave his whole life to making possible.

3. Pray this prayer: *"Lord, help me be faithful in the small things, day after day, when no one is watching."*

Feast Day

August 4 — St. John Vianney is the patron saint of priests and parish priests in particular. His feast is widely celebrated in seminaries and parishes around the world, and his incorrupt body remains in the basilica at Ars, France.

CHAPTER 47

St. Maximilian Kolbe

The Priest Who Said "Take Me Instead"

"He stepped forward in Auschwitz and asked to die in a stranger's place."

Martyr of Auschwitz | Virtue: Sacrifice & Charity

The Story

In the summer of 1941, a prisoner escaped from Auschwitz.

The Nazi policy was immediate: ten men from the escaped prisoners' block would be selected at random and starved to death in an underground bunker. The guards made their selection. One of the men chosen, a Polish sergeant named Franciszek

Gajowniczek, cried out that he had a wife and children.

A priest in the line stepped forward.

"I would like to take this man's place," said Maximilian Kolbe. "I am old and not much use to anyone." He was forty-seven. The SS commander stared at him, then nodded.

Kolbe was a Franciscan priest who had been arrested in 1941 for publishing material critical of the Nazi occupation and sheltering thousands of Jews and refugees at his friary. He arrived at Auschwitz in May of that year. He continued ministering to fellow prisoners in the camp, hearing confessions, leading prayer, and giving away his food rations to those who needed them more.

In the starvation bunker, witnesses who survived reported that Kolbe led the other condemned men in prayer and hymns. He comforted the dying. After two weeks, he was the only one still alive. The guards administered a lethal injection to finish the process. He died on August 14, 1941, holding out his arm to make it easier for the executioner.

Franciszek Gajowniczek, the man whose place he had taken, survived the war. He attended Kolbe's canonization in 1982, where Pope John Paul II, himself Polish, called Kolbe a martyr of charity. Gajowniczek died in 1995 at the age of ninety-three.

Virtue Spotlight: Sacrifice & Charity

Sacrifice means giving up something you cannot get back for someone else's sake. Kolbe gave everything.

Charity is what made him step forward. He looked at a stranger and decided that man's life mattered more than his own.

In your life: You are not being asked to die for anyone. But you are asked, every day, to put someone else's needs before your own comfort. That is where Kolbe's love starts.

Remember This

Love is not a feeling. It is a decision made in a specific moment, often at a cost.

Hero Mission

1. Give something up today for someone else's sake: your seat, your time, your turn.

2. Learn more about Auschwitz and what happened there. Understanding history is part of making sure it doesn't repeat.

3. Pray this prayer: *"Lord, help me love others the way You love me – completely, without holding back."*

Feast Day

August 14 — St. Maximilian Kolbe's feast falls on the eve of the Assumption of Mary, a feast he had a particular devotion to throughout his life. He is the patron saint of prisoners, journalists, and those who struggle with addiction.

CHAPTER 48

St. Pier Giorgio Frassati

The Mountain Climber Who Served the Poor

"He climbed the Alps on weekends. On weekdays, he carried the sick up staircases."

Man of the Beatitudes | Virtue: Charity & Joy

The Story

Pier Giorgio Frassati was the kind of person everyone wanted to be around.

He was twenty-four when he died, a university student in Turin, Italy, the son of a wealthy and prominent family. He was tall, athletic, and deeply funny. He organized mountain-climbing trips with his friends, played pranks, loved music, and had a gift for making whoever he was with feel like the most interesting person in the room.

He also spent most of his free time in Turin's poorest neighborhoods.

He was a member of the St. Vincent de Paul Society and the Third Order of Dominicans, and he took both seriously. He visited the sick and elderly in their homes, climbing multiple flights of stairs in tenement buildings to reach people who couldn't come to him. He gave away his bus fare and walked home. He gave away his coat. When his friends gave him money as a gift, it was gone within days, spent on medicine or food for someone in the neighborhood.

He kept it quiet. His own family had no idea how extensive his charitable work was until after he died.

In the summer of 1925, Pier Giorgio contracted poliomyelitis, likely from handling patients in his visits to the sick. He kept visiting until he couldn't move. He died on July 4, 1925. At his funeral, his family expected a modest gathering. Instead, the streets of Turin were filled with the poor, the sick, and the people he had served, faces his family had never seen, who had come to say goodbye to someone who had changed their lives.

Pope John Paul II beatified him in 1990 and called him a man of the Beatitudes. He was canonized on April 27, 2025, alongside St. Carlo Acutis.

Virtue Spotlight: Charity & Joy

Charity in Pier Giorgio was entirely natural. He didn't distinguish between his social life and his service.

They were the same thing.

Joy is what happens when you stop treating faith as an obligation and start treating it as an adventure.

In your life: Can you think of one way to combine something you enjoy with something that helps others? That integration is exactly what Pier Giorgio lived.

Remember This

Holiness is not something you add to your life. It's something you pour into everything you're already doing.

Hero Mission

1. Do something fun with a friend this week, and find one way to make it an act of service as well.

2. Give something away this week without telling anyone, and don't expect it back.

3. Pray this prayer: *"Lord, help me live fully and generously, so that my life looks like joy and love at the same time."*

Feast Day

July 4 — St. Pier Giorgio Frassati's feast day is celebrated on the anniversary of his death. He was canonized on April 27, 2025, the same day as St. Carlo Acutis, and is venerated by young Catholics around the world as a model of joyful, active faith.

NOTES

CHAPTER 49

St. Thérèse of Lisieux

The Little Flower's Big Secret

"She died at 24 in a small convent. The Pope called her the greatest saint of modern times."

Doctor of the Church | Virtue: Humility & Love

The Story

Thérèse Martin entered a Carmelite convent in Normandy, France, at the age of fifteen and never left.

She was the youngest of five sisters, four of whom became nuns. She had been a sensitive, intense child who cried easily and wanted everything with her whole heart. She also wanted to be a great saint. She read the lives of the martyrs and felt that longing burn in her. She wanted to do heroic things for God.

She was a laundress in a small convent in Lisieux. She swept floors. She prayed. She was kind to the sisters who irritated her, which was not always easy. She got tuberculosis and died at twenty-four.

And yet she discovered something in that small, hidden life that she called the "Little Way," a path to holiness built not on dramatic gestures but on ordinary moments done with extraordinary love—the small act of kindness. The duty done cheerfully when you don't feel like it. The irritation swallowed quietly. The prayer offered in the dark when nothing feels real.

She wrote about it in her autobiography, which she completed just before she died, at her prioress's request. She called it Story of a Soul. It was published after her death, and within a few years, it had spread across the world. By 1925, thirty years after her death, she was canonized. Pope Pius X, who had read her book, called her the greatest saint of modern times.

She had said, just before she died: "I will spend my heaven doing good on earth." She is one of the most invoked saints in the world.

Virtue Spotlight: Humility & Love

Humility doesn't mean thinking less of yourself. It means being exactly who you are, fully and without performance.

Love in Thérèse's sense was the willingness to do the smallest things with complete attention and genuine care.

In your life: What small thing could you do today with more care than you normally give it? That is the Little Way. Anyone can practice it.

Remember This

You don't have to do great things. You have to do small things with great love.

Hero Mission

1. Choose one ordinary task today, making your bed, washing a dish, saying hello to someone,e and do it as well and as cheerfully as you possibly can.

2. Read one chapter of Story of a Soul if you can find it. It was written for people your age to understand.

3. Pray this prayer: *"Lord, help me find You in the small things, and love You there."*

Feast Day

October 1 — St. Thérèse of Lisieux is the patron saint of missionaries, France, and those who are sick. She is a Doctor of the Church, one of only four women to hold that title, and her roses, her promised sign from heaven, are still reported by devoted people around the world.

CHAPTER 50

St. Carlo Acutis

The Teen Who Put God Online

"He built a website about Eucharistic miracles at 12. He died at 15. Canonized 2025."

First Millennial Saint | Virtue: Faith & Zeal

The Story

Carlo Acutis was born in London in 1991, grew up in Milan, and loved video games, his cat, and the Eucharist, roughly in that order of intensity.

He was an ordinary Italian teenager who went to school, played football, programmed computers, and spent time with friends.
He was also, by any measure, unusually serious about his faith.
He attended Mass every day from the

time he could choose to do so on his own. He said the Eucharist was his highway to heaven, and he meant it literally.

At twelve years old, he decided to document Eucharistic miracles, the reported instances throughout Church history where the consecrated bread and wine had shown signs that could not be explained naturally, bleeding hosts, preserved incorruptible flesh, healings tied to specific expositions of the Blessed Sacrament. He gathered the cases, researched each one, and built a website to catalog them so that anyone in the world could access the information for free.

He completed the project. He never used it to get attention for himself. He said it was for God.

In 2006, at fifteen years old, Carlo was diagnosed with an aggressive form of leukemia. He was told it was terminal. His response, recorded by his family and friends, was characteristic: he offered his suffering to God for the Pope and for the Church, and asked that others not have to endure what he was going through. He died on October 3, 2006.

He was beatified in 2020. His body was found to be incorrupt. He was canonized on April 27, 2025, becoming the first millennial saint in the history of the Catholic Church.

His website is still online.

Virtue Spotlight: Faith & Zeal

Faith in Carlo looked like daily Mass, consistent prayer, and the conviction that what he believed was worth his best work.

Zeal means channeling what you're good at into what you love most. Carlo was good at computers. He used them for God.

In your life: What are you good at? What do you spend your time on? Carlo's question, which he answered clearly, is worth asking yourself: how could those things be offered back to God?

Remember This

You don't have to be an adult to begin. Carlo was twelve. You have everything you need right now.

Hero Mission

1. Visit Carlo's website on Eucharistic miracles and read about one case that interests you.
2. Go to Mass this week with the intention of paying more attention than usual to what is happening.
3. Pray this prayer: *"Lord, show me how to use what I have right now to love You better."*

Feast Day

October 12 — St. Carlo Acutis's feast day. He is the patron saint of the internet, young people, and those who use technology, a reminder that every tool can be offered to God.

Feast Day Calender - 50 Days

● Male saint ● Female saint

JANUARY 4

Jan 20	● St. Sebastian	Soldier & Martyr
Jan 21	● St. Agnes	Patron of Girls & Purity
Jan 28	● St. Thomas Aquinas	Doctor of the Church
Jan 31	● St. John Bosco	Patron of Youth

FEBRUARY 3

Feb 10	● Bl. José Sánchez del Rio	Cristero Martyr, age 14
Feb 10	● St. Scholastica	Sister of St. Benedict
Feb 23	● St. Polycarp	Bishop & Martyr

MARCH 5

Mar 7	● St. Perpetua	Martyr of Carthage
Mar 9	● St. Dominic Savio	Patron of Youth, age 14
Mar 17	● St. Patrick	Apostle of Ireland
Mar 19	● St. Joseph	Patron of the Universal Church
Mar 22	● St. Nicholas Owen	Carpenter Martyr

APRIL 1

Apr 23	● St. George	Patron of England

MAY 5

May 10	● St. Damien of Molokai	Apostle of Lepers
May 16	● St. Brendan the Navigator	Explorer Monk
May 22	● St. Rita of Cascia	Patron of Impossible Causes
May 26	● St. Philip Neri	Apostle of Rome
May 30	● St. Joan of Arc	Patron of France

JUNE 7

Jun 5	● St. Boniface	Apostle of Germany
Jun 13	● St. Anthony of Padua	Finder of Lost Things
Jun 21	● St. Aloysius Gonzaga	Patron of Youth
Jun 22	● St. Thomas More	Patron of Lawyers
Jun 22	● St. John Fisher	Bishop & Martyr
Jun 29	● St. Peter	First Pope
Jun 29	● St. Paul	Apostle to the Gentiles

JULY 2

Jul 1	● Bl. Junipero Serra	Franciscan Missionary
Jul 3	● St. Thomas the Apostle	Apostle to India

www.ingramcontent.com/pod-product-compliance
Lightning Source LLC
LaVergne TN
LVHW010915110826
845149LV00013B/2369

* 9 7 9 8 9 9 2 6 0 7 6 1 1 *